JAZZ piano HANDBOOK

essential jazz piano skills for all musicians

michele WEIR

Alfred

GERSHWIN® and GEORGE GERSHWIN® are registered trademarks of Gershwin Enterprises
IRA GERSHWIN™ is a trademark of Gershwin Enterprises

© 2008 BELWIN-MILLS PUBLISHING CORP., A Division of ALFRED PUBLISHING CO., INC.

IS THIS BOOK FOR ME?

If you are....

- a jazz singer or instrumentalist who recognizes that jazz piano skills are a must

- a private or classroom teacher of jazz who is motivated to become more effective

- a pianist (classical, pop or other) who is interested in jazz and enthusiastic about a practical approach to playing it

...then this book is for you!

WHAT WILL I LEARN?

- Open any fake book or sheet music with chord symbols and be able to play a tune.

- Teach your student how to play a tune by demonstrating it at the piano.

- Accompany yourself or another vocalist or instrumentalist on any type of tune – swing, ballad, Latin or other.

- Get a solo piano/vocal gig.

- Use the piano as a helpful tool to practice vocal improvisation.

- Analyze the chord changes to a song and understand the function of each chord within the progression.

- Double-check published leads-sheets for accuracy, or creatively embellish your own.

- Improve your composition skills by being able to play and hear the tunes you write.

- Improve your improvisation skills by understanding the harmonic construction of a song.

- Impress family or friends by playing and singing a song at the next party or get together.

- Become a better-educated singer, instrumentalist or teacher of jazz, with a thorough understanding of the music and the confidence that goes along with it.

You'll never regret the time you take to acquire these skills!

Michele Weir

ABOUT THE AUTHOR

Michele Weir is one of the leading figures in vocal jazz education today. She has earned international recognition through a diverse set of talents as teacher, arranger, singer and pianist.

Currently serving on the faculty of University of California, Los Angeles, Michele has previously taught at the University of Southern California, CSU Long Beach and the Phil Mattson School. Highly respected as a teacher and clinician, her work has taken her to more than 22 countries around the globe. Recent notable presentations include the World Choral Symposium, the IAJE Conference, and the ACDA National Conference.

With dozens of published vocal arrangements to her credit, plus works for big band and orchestra, Michele is a prolific arranger. Professional ensembles performing her work include Beachfront Property, M-Pact, New York Voices, Chanticleer, Voice Trek, the Boston Pops, and the Buffalo, Cincinnati and Pacific Symphonies. Michele's music has been featured on the Shari Lewis TV show, Disney's "101 Dalmatians" sing-along CD, and the Holland America Cruise Line. Her previously published books, Vocal Improvisation (Advance Music) and Jazz Singer's Handbook (Alfred Publishing) are available worldwide.

A former member of the Grammy-nominated vocal group, Phil Mattson and the PM Singers, Michele frequently performs as featured guest vocalist at educational jazz festivals. As a pianist, she has toured extensively with a variety of artists, including singer Bobby Vinton. In her role as Music Supervisor for the DreamWorks film Prince of Egypt, she journeyed through Europe and Asia overseeing music production for the film's foreign language dubs.

In 2004, Michele launched an online publishing company, MichMusic (www.michmusic.com). Her solo CD with jazz guitarist Bruce Forman is titled "The Sound of Music."

www.micheleweir.com

www.michmusic.com

ACKNOWLEDGMENTS

Special thanks to everyone who generously contributed their thoughts and ideas to this project: Jennifer Barnes, Kevin Burke, Jack Daro, Rosana Eckert, Greg Jasperse, and Kristin Korb.

Contents

ABOVE AND BEYOND

CD Track Listing

Listening is critical! A demonstration CD is included to provide a model for how the exercises should sound when played correctly, musically and with good piano technique.

Track	Title	Chapter	Exercise	Focus
1	Emily; You'd Be So Nice to Come Home To	2	Exercises 16 and 19 (Pages 26 and 30)	Voicing and Pattern P1
2	Emily; You'd Be So Nice to Come Home To	3	Exercises 24 and 27 (Pages 36 and 39)	Voicing and Pattern P2
3	Emily; You'd Be So Nice to Come Home To	4	Exercises 28 and 29 (Pages 41 and 42)	Voicing and Patterns P1 and P2 combined
4	East of the Sun	5	Exercise 32 (Page 55)	Swing "2" and "4" feels
5	Gentle Rain	5	Exercise 34 (Page 59)	Bossa Nova
6	The Shadow of Your Smile	6	Exercise 41 (Page 75)	Five-note voicings with color notes
7	The Shadow of Your Smile	7	Exercise 45a and 45b (Pages 84 and 85)	Voicing and Patterns P1, P2, P3 and P4 combined
8	The Shadow of Your Smile	8	Exercise 47 (Page 92)	Five-note open voicings
9	The Shadow of Your Smile	9	Exercise 50 (Page 101)	Broken chords and passing notes
10	You Go To My Head	10	Exercise 52 (Page106)	Playing the song's melody
11	Rainy Day	Appendix I	Etude 1 (Page 111)	Patterns P1 and P2 combined; block chords (Chapter 4)
12	You Love Me	Appendix 1	Etude 2 (Page 112)	Patterns P1 and P2 combined; block chords (Chapter 4)
13	The Moon Has Risen	Appendix I	Etude 3 (Page 113)	Swing "2" and "4" feel (Chapter 5)
14	Lullaby for the Birds	Appendix 1	Etude 4 (Page 114)	Swing "2" and "4" feel (Chapter 5)
15	A Fool's Day	Appendix 1	Etude 5 (Page 115)	Bossa Nova (Chapter 5)
16	In Love I Will Fall	Appendix 1	Etude 6 (Page 116)	Ballad tempo (Chapter 5)
17	Time and Time Again	Appendix 1	Etude 7 (Page 117)	Patterns P1 and P2 combined with five-note, block chord voicings and color notes (Chapter 6)
18	Far Away a Long Time Ago	Appendix 1	Etude 8 (Page 118)	Patterns P1, P2, P3 and P4 combined with five-note, block chord voicings and color notes (Chapter 7)
19	What Could Be New?	Appendix 1	Etude 9 (Page 119)	Five-note open voicings (Chapter 8)
20	Don't Tell Me	Appendix 1	Etude 10 (Page 120)	Five-note open voicings (Chapter 8)
21	You Are All Things	Appendix 1	Etude 11 (Page 121)	Broken chords and passing notes (Chapter 9)
22	Valentine's Day	Appendix 1	Etude 12 (Page 122)	Broken chords and passing notes (Chapter 9)
23	Embraceable You	Appendix 1	Etude 13 (Page 123)	Playing the melody (Chapter 10)
24	A Foggy Day	Appendix 1	Etude 14 (Page 124)	Playing the melody (Chapter 10)

ABOUT THIS BOOK

This publication will provide you with the tools to be able to sit at the piano and play the chord changes to tunes, simple as that! You may not end up sounding like the legendary jazz pianist Oscar Peterson, but you will gain the piano skills necessary to becoming a more well-rounded and competent jazz singer, player or teacher. I guarantee the time you devote now to learning basic jazz piano is something you'll never regret!

1. The chapters of this book are separated in to two sections: **The Essentials** and **Above and Beyond**.

   - **The Essentials** is the study and practice of basic voicings and their application to songs.

   - **Above and Beyond** will expand your skills and knowledge with the addition of more sophisticated voicings, color notes, a more pianistic style of playing, and skills to harmonize a melody.

   - **Appendices I and II** are resources for practice etudes and additional information.

2. Exercises are progressive and designed to be followed in chronological order.

3. You will need what is commonly known as a fake book to apply the piano techniques you'll learn to songs. I highly recommend the *Just Standards Real Book*, (Alfred Publishing), *Just Jazz Real Book*, (Alfred Publishing), or *The Standards Real Book* (Sher Music Company). Each of these books contain hundreds of great songs and the chord changes are complete and correct. There are numerous others available as well.

4. The following symbols occur throughout the book and will indicate an action:
   to Play, Listen or Study.

 • Play: Exercise    • Listen To: CD Track    • Study: Example

MUSICAL PREREQUISITES

To use this book, you *do not* need to be an accomplished pianist with seven years of study at Juilliard! However, you *do* need to have basic familiarity with the piano and a solid understanding of music fundamentals, to include the following:

- Key and meter signatures

- Major and minor scales

- Intervals

- Triads—major, minor, augmented, diminished

- Understanding and counting basic rhythms

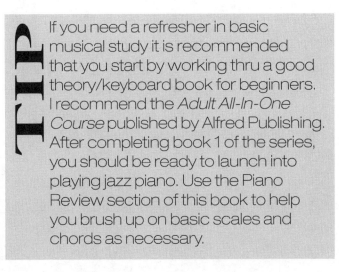
TIP

If you need a refresher in basic musical study it is recommended that you start by working thru a good theory/keyboard book for beginners. I recommend the *Adult All-In-One Course* published by Alfred Publishing. After completing book 1 of the series, you should be ready to launch into playing jazz piano. Use the Piano Review section of this book to help you brush up on basic scales and chords as necessary.

> If you have no prior piano playing experience, it is essential that you work through the Piano Review section before beginning the exercises in this book.

THE REALITY OF PRACTICE

The fact that you're reading this section is a good sign! Jazz piano skills cannot be acquired by simply reading a book; they require practice. For some people, the idea of devoting significant time to practice is daunting. But, practice is very palatable if done in bite-sized steps, and it can be a lot of fun, especially after the early stages. Set a personal goal of 20–30 minutes a day for practice. If time allows you to do more, great, but plan on following through with your personal (minimum) goal.

- Effective practice takes careful repetition, repetition, repetition, of the correct notes. **It is counterproductive to repeatedly practice something if you're making mistakes.** Work slowly at first, making sure you're playing all exercises correctly.

- Work toward a combination of the following goals in your practice:

  o Cognitive understanding: **know** what needs to be played

  o Muscle memory development: **feel** the chords and train your hands to remember the feeling

  o Ear training: **hear** the chords and become familiar with the different sounds

Just like anything else in life, the real key to success in learning jazz piano is committing to do it. Once you're committed to this goal, you will naturally want to study and practice because you know you have to in order to meet your goal. So it boils down to this simple question: do you want to learn to play jazz piano, or not?

Before You Begin: Piano Review

GOAL: Work on basic piano skills including scales and chords. The exercises in this chapter will help you in the development finger dexterity, two-hand coordination and the technique required to play well-balanced chords. Practicing the exercises in all keys will give you a visual and kinesthetic awareness of each different key center.

Piano Review is designed to assist non-pianists in gaining basic piano facility. *It is essential that you have basic piano facility prior to beginning Chapter 1 of this book.* Even if you already have a piano background, please take a look at the exercises in this section to determine if you need to brush-up on your skills. If you can already play each of the exercises in this section correctly and at the suggested tempo markings, then you're ready to start on Chapter 1.

TECHNIQUE BASICS

Most physical endeavors, such as tennis, ballet, or piano playing, require a delicate balance of exertion and relaxation. Depending on the activity, certain muscles need to be active while others should remain uninvolved and relaxed. Ideally, the muscles that are active should work efficiently by doing their job without excess exertion or strain. With this in mind, if you feel tension in fingers, arms, or shoulders when playing piano, it is a signal that something needs adjustment.

Consider these tips regarding healthy piano technique:

1. Keep your wrists straight and relaxed. This may require you to move your torso closer to or further away from the piano until you feel comfortable and your elbows are slightly forward without feeling cramped in too close.

2. Shoulders should stay down and arms relaxed. Keep your wrists approximately at the same level as the white keys.

3. Hands should be relaxed with fingers slightly curved, as if you're comfortably holding an orange. Play on the tips of the fingers. It's difficult to play the piano with long fingernails!

4. Fingers should move independently. When one finger depresses a note, the others should stay relaxed, gently resting on the keyboard. This can be tricky if you're new to piano playing.

Diagram 1: Good posture

Diagram 2: Poor posture

TIP
For purposes of this book, you're not required to maintain an ongoing practice regimen for piano technique. However, you may find it helpful to occasionally brush up on your technique by revisiting the exercises in this section.

FIVE-NOTE WARMUP

Exercises 1 and 2 should be played as written with both hands together at the same time. Your two hands should play in perfect sync with the notes of the chords sounding at the same time with equal pianistic weight. Remember that fingers should be above the keyboard and slightly curved. All five fingers of each hand should rest gently in position on their respective notes. Practice with a metronome until you can play the exercises at ♩ = 80. It's okay to start slower at first and gradually increase the tempo. If you find the exercise difficult, try playing with the hands separately, then gradually put the two hands together.

PLAY Exercise 1
Major

Exercise 2
Minor

SCALES

In this section you'll practice major and minor scales in all keys. Example 1 illustrates three types of minor scales associated with traditional music theory.

STUDY **Example 1**

Each natural minor scale corresponds to a relative major scale that shares the same notes and key signature. For example, the D minor scale contains the same notes and key signature as the F major scale. D minor is referred to as the *relative minor* of F major and conversely, F major is the *relative major* of D minor.

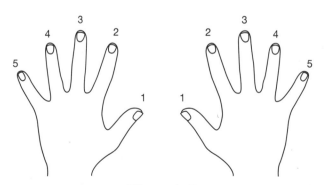

Diagram 3
Fingering Chart

DIATONIC TRIADS

Diatonic triads are three-note chords built on each degree of a given scale, using notes from within that scale.

Play Exercise 5 in all keys with your right hand only. Practice this exercise until you can play it at ♩ = 63.

Exercise 5

USE OF THE DAMPER PEDAL

The *damper pedal*, otherwise known as the sustain pedal, is the foot pedal located on the far right. Use of the damper pedal helps to connect the chords smoothly in legato playing.

If you are a non-pianist and have no experience in using the damper pedal, try the following exercise: Using the diatonic triads from Exercise 5, depress the damper pedal with your right foot just after playing the first chord. Then lift your hand up from the keyboard while continuing to hold the pedal down. Play the next chord and release the damper pedal at the same time. Then, immediately depress the pedal again, repeating the process for each of the chords in the exercise. Going through every key will give your foot a fairly good work-out!

Exercise 2
Minor

Exercise 4
Natural Minor Scales

*ALL L.H. SCALES SHOULD BE PLAYED 8VB.

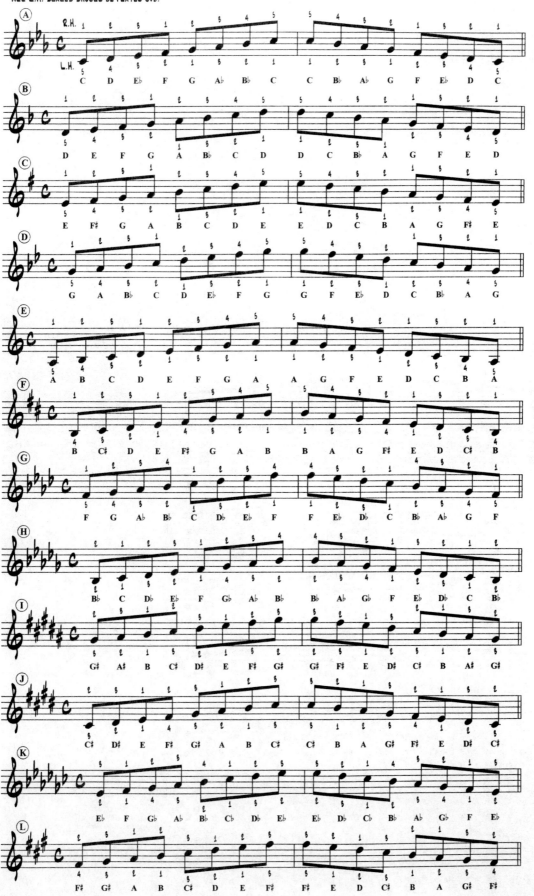

TIP

For right hand fingering in scales, the thumb should cross *under* the hand when ascending, and fingers should cross *over* the thumb when descending. The reverse is true for left hand scales: fingers cross *over* the thumb when ascending and the thumb crosses *under* when descending.

SCALES

In this section you'll practice major and minor scales in all keys. Example 1 illustrates three types of minor scales associated with traditional music theory.

STUDY **Example 1**

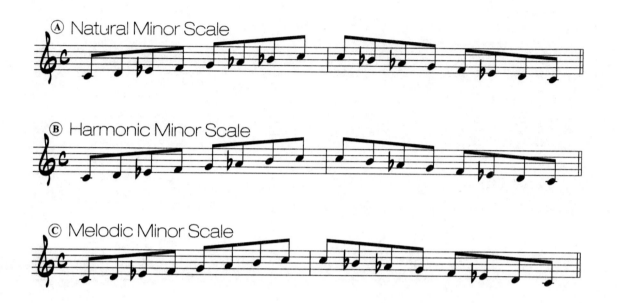

Ⓐ Natural Minor Scale

Ⓑ Harmonic Minor Scale

Ⓒ Melodic Minor Scale

Each natural minor scale corresponds to a relative major scale that shares the same notes and key signature. For example, the D minor scale contains the same notes and key signature as the F major scale. D minor is referred to as the *relative minor* of F major and conversely, F major is the *relative major* of D minor.

Diagram 3
Fingering Chart

L.H. R.H.
E   G

R.H.   R.H.   R.H.   R.H. R.H.
| | | | 2 | | |
    L.H. L. L.H. L.H. R.i'

R.H. ⟶
2 2 4 2 2 | |

R.H.
| | | 2 | | |
   L.H. L.H L.H. L.H.
              R.H. R.H.

R.H R.H. R.H.
2 2 | 3 | 2 3
         L.H. ⟶

R.H   R.H.
| | | 2 4 | | 3 | 2
   L.H. l   L.H. ⟶

R.H | | R.H 2 4   2 | 3 | 2 3
   L.H   L.H.

FIVE-NOTE WARMUP

Exercise 1
Major

Exercises 1 and 2 should be played as written with both hands together at the same time. Your two hands should play in perfect sync with the notes of the chords sounding at the same time with equal pianistic weight. Remember that fingers should be above the keyboard and slightly curved. All five fingers of each hand should rest gently in position on their respective notes. Practice with a metronome until you can play the exercises at ♩ = 80. It's okay to start slower at first and gradually increase the tempo. If you find the exercise difficult, try playing with the hands separately, then gradually put the two hands together.

Play Exercises 3 and 4 with your dominant hand only. (Use your left if you're left handed, and your right if you're right handed.) Practice with the metronome until you can play the scales at ♩ = 63. As with Exercises 1 and 2, it's OK to start slowly at first and gradually increase the tempo. The order of key centers of these exercises was designed so that scales with the same or similar fingerings would be played in succession. *Be sure to use the indicated fingerings written above each note as in Diagram 3.*

Exercise 3
Major Scales

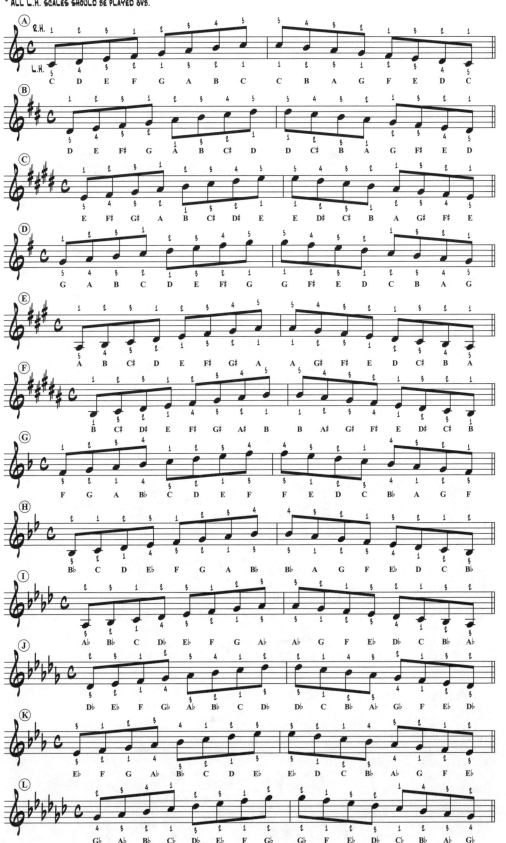

* ALL L.H. SCALES SHOULD BE PLAYED 8VB.

Optionally, practice Exercises 3 and 4 with both hands together to develop your two-handed coordination.

Exercise 4
Natural Minor Scales

* ALL L.H. SCALES SHOULD BE PLAYED 8VB.

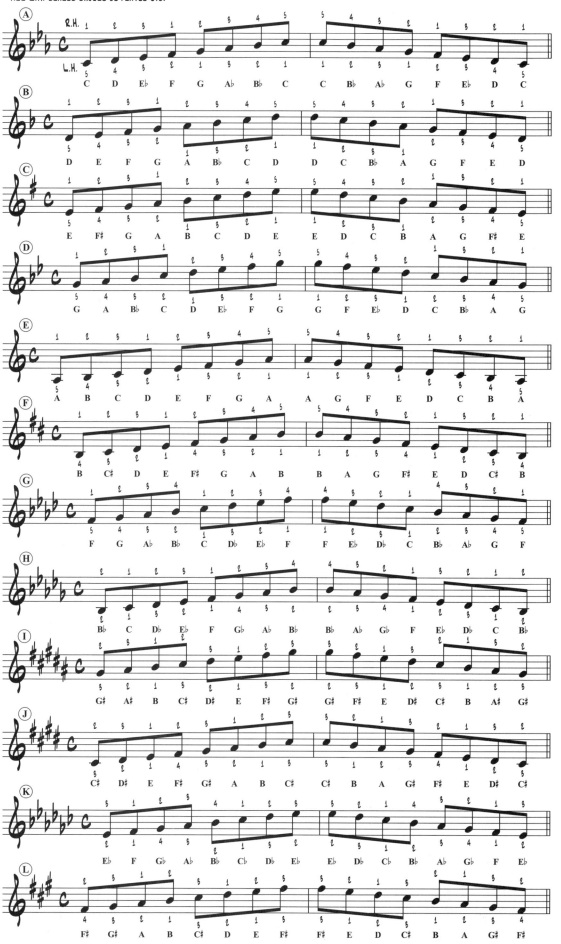

TIP

For right hand fingering in scales, the thumb should cross *under* the hand when ascending, and fingers should cross *over* the thumb when descending. The reverse is true for left hand scales: fingers cross *over* the thumb when ascending and the thumb crosses *under* when descending.

DIATONIC TRIADS

Diatonic triads are three-note chords built on each degree of a given scale, using notes from within that scale.

Play Exercise 5 in all keys with your right hand only. Practice this exercise until you can play it at ♩ = 63.

Exercise 5

USE OF THE DAMPER PEDAL

The *damper pedal*, otherwise known as the sustain pedal, is the foot pedal located on the far right. Use of the damper pedal helps to connect the chords smoothly in legato playing.

If you are a non-pianist and have no experience in using the damper pedal, try the following exercise: Using the diatonic triads from Exercise 5, depress the damper pedal with your right foot just after playing the first chord. Then lift your hand up from the keyboard while continuing to hold the pedal down. Play the next chord and release the damper pedal at the same time. Then, immediately depress the pedal again, repeating the process for each of the chords in the exercise. Going through every key will give your foot a fairly good work-out!

Chapter 1 Jazz Piano 101

The Essentials

> **GOAL:** Study the circle of fifths for use in identifying key signatures and analyzing jazz chord progressions. Learn the five chord types that are most common in jazz: major 7th, dominant 7th, minor 7th, minor 7th, ♭5 and diminished 7th and practice them in all keys. Get an overview of the primary voicings that will be used throughout this book: P1, P2, P3, and P4.

CIRCLE OF FIFTHS

The *circle of 5ths* gets its name from the fact that as you go from one chord to the next in the circle, you are going up or down by an interval of a (perfect) 5th. If you go *up* a 5th (clockwise), the key has one more sharp or one less flat; if you go *down* a 5th (counterclockwise), the key has one more flat or one less sharp. Diagram 4 illustrates the most common harmonic movement in jazz standard chord progressions: movement to the left (counterclockwise) in the circle of 5ths.

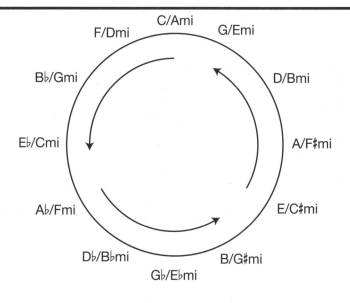

Diagram 4

CHORD TYPES

There are four chord families: major, dominant, minor and diminished. Within the four chord families, there are numerous types of chords used in jazz standards. These chords usually consist of a triad plus an added 7th or 6th.

Diagram 5 illustrates all standard jazz chord types in the key of C, along with their corresponding chord symbols.

Diagram 5

Major Family			Dominant Family		Minor Family					Diminished Family	
Major Triad	Major Sixth	Major Seventh	Dominant Seventh	Dominant Seventh Sus	Minor Triad	Minor Sixth	Minor Seventh	Minor Seventh Flat 5	Minor/ Major Seventh	Diminished Triad	Diminished Seventh
C	C6	CMA7	C7	C7SUS	CMI	CMI6	CMI7	CMI7(♭5)	CMI(MA7)	C○	C○7
1, 3, 5	1, 3, 5, 6	1, 3, 5, 7	1, 3, 6, ♭7	1, 4, 5, ♭7	1, ♭3, 5	1, ♭3, 5, ♭7	1, ♭3, 5, ♭7	1, ♭3, ♭5, ♭7	1, ♭3, 5, 7	1, ♭3, ♭5	1, ♭3. ♭5, ♭♭7

You may encounter a variety of different chord symbols used to represent the same chord in other publications because there is currently no standardization for chord symbol nomenclature. Each musician has their own chord symbol preferences. Refer to Appendix II for a complete catalog of chord types and corresponding chord symbols.

The five most commonly used jazz chord types are major 7th, dominant 7th, minor 7th, minor 7th, ♭5, and diminished 7th. Familiarity with each of these chord types is fundamental to playing jazz piano. Practice Exercises 6—10 as written (in all 12 keys). Your goal is to be able to play them perfectly at ♩=80. Notice that some of the chords in Exercises 9 and 10 use enharmonic spellings to make the chords easier to read. Be sure to *begin* your practice exercises in a different key each day. Avoid starting in the key of C all the time to ensure fluency in *all* the keys!

Exercise 6
Major Seventh Chords

Exercise 7
Dominant Seventh Chords

Exercise 8
Minor Seventh Chords

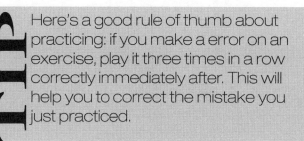

TIP

Here's a good rule of thumb about practicing: if you make a error on an exercise, play it three times in a row correctly immediately after. This will help you to correct the mistake you just practiced.

Exercise 9
Minor Seventh, Flat Five Chords

Exercise 10
Diminished Seventh Chords

INTRO TO VOICINGS

QUICK-FIX VOICING

A *voicing* is the arrangement of notes in a chord. Jazz pianists utilize a wide variety of voicing types to maintain interest in their playing. Voicing configurations can range from simple and sparse to very complex and dense.

The *Quick-Fix* voicing is just what the name suggests, an easy way to make the chords you already know have a more interesting jazz flavor by changing the order of notes. Think of the Quick-Fix voicing as a default voicing allowing you to play songs even with minimal jazz piano experience. You will probably not use the Quick-Fix voicing as a regular part of your piano playing, but for now, it will help you navigate through tunes in a jazz style.

The Quick-Fix voicing consists of the 3rd and 7th of each chord (or 3rd and 6th as dictated by the chord symbol) in the right hand, and the root of the chord in the left. It is derived from the *block chords* in Exercises 6-10. (*Block chords* are four-note chords voiced in close position with all notes played at the same time, not arpeggiated.) The Quick-Fix voicing is often referred to as a *shell voicing*.

STUDY Example 2

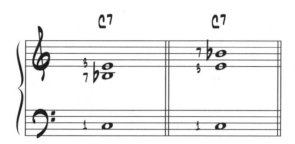

Exercise 11 illustrates how the Quick-Fix voicing can be applied to a jazz standard song. Practice it until you can play it easily with no mistakes. Play the bottom two staves only; the song's melody is provided only for your reference. Notice that the right hand 3rds and 7ths are inverted as needed to minimize the repositioning of hands.

Exercise 11
"I Got Rhythm"

Music and Lyrics by
GEORGE GERSHWIN and IRA GERSHWIN

Additional Practice:

Try out the Quick-Fix voicing in other tunes of your choice. Good song choices include "All the Things You Are," and "I Can't Get Started." As in Exercise 11, invert the right hand 3rds and 7ths as needed to minimize the repositioning of hands as much as possible. This will allow for a smooth, linear connection between chords. Keep your right hand notes in the middle range of the keyboard.

VOICINGS OVERVIEW

There are four primary voicings you'll study and practice throughout this book: Voicings P1 (Position #1), P2 (Position #2), P3 (Position #3) and P4 (Position #4). Once you have command of these four key voicings and their variations, you'll be equipped to play jazz piano like a pro.

Chapters 2-5 will deal exclusively with Voicings P1 and P2 in a four-note configuration. A good way to help you remember each voicing is to *associate it with the top note of the chord*. Example 3 illustrates Voicing P1 (5th on top) and Voicing P2 (3rd on top).

 **Example 3**

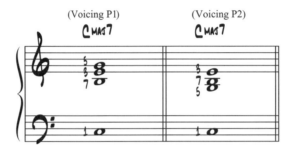

In Chapter 6, you'll be introduced to Voicings P3 and P4 in a five-note configuration. Again, it's a good idea to associate each voicing with the top note of the chord. Voicing P3 (9th on top) and Voicing P4 (7th on top) are illustrated in Example 4. Notice in both chord voicings that the chord symbol Cmaj9 is used to indicate a major 7th chord with added *9th*. (The 9th is the same as the 2nd scale degree and is referred to as an *extension*. Extensions are notes commonly added to chords for color. You'll study more about extensions in Chapter 6).

 **Example 4**

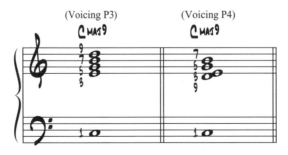

In the second half of the book, **Above and Beyond**, you'll learn to use a combination of all four voicings to achieve interest and variety in your playing. Voicings P1, P2, P3 and P4 work in conjunction with chord progression Patterns P1, P2, P3 and P4.

Chapter 2 Position #1 (P1)

> **GOAL:** Study and practice Voicing P1 and its related chord progression pattern, Pattern P1 and apply them to chord types and jazz standard songs. Understand and become comfortable with the ii-V-I chord progression in all major and minor keys. This is essential harmonic information for all jazz pianists.

VOICING P1 (MAJOR, DOMINANT AND MINOR SEVENTH CHORDS)

The notes in Voicing P1 are (from the bottom up) the root, 7th (or the 6th), 3rd and 5th of any chord. Example 5 illustrates Voicing P1 applied to major, dominant and minor 7th chords. Note that the 5th is the top note of the voicing.

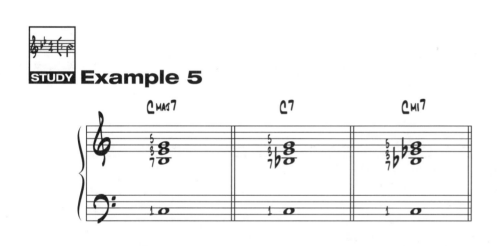

STUDY Example 5

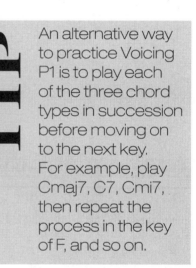

TIP An alternative way to practice Voicing P1 is to play each of the three chord types in succession before moving on to the next key. For example, play Cmaj7, C7, Cmi7, then repeat the process in the key of F, and so on.

Exercises 12-14 take Voicing P1 through all keys with major, dominant and minor 7th chords. Your goal is to be able to play them perfectly at ♩=80. Though the exercises are written out in all keys, play the chords without reading them after your first few practice sessions.

PLAY Exercise 12
Major Seventh Chords

Exercise 13
Dominant Seventh Chords

Exercise 14
Minor Seventh Chords

THE ii-V-I PROGRESSION

If you've spent much time around jazz musicians, you've probably already heard of the ii-V-I progression. The vast majority of jazz standards contain at least several episodes of the complete or *partial* (ii-V) ii-V-I progression. This progression is contained within an important and slightly longer progression commonly used in intros, endings, and *turnarounds*, I-vi-ii-V-I. Turnarounds are short progressions that often occur at the end of a song to provide a harmonic link back to the beginning of the song.

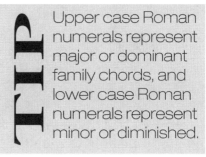

TIP

Upper case Roman numerals represent major or dominant family chords, and lower case Roman numerals represent minor or diminished.

Example 6 illustrates 7th chords built from the major scale and their corresponding Roman numerals. These chords are *diatonic*, meaning, they are comprised of notes that occur naturally (no alteration) within the scale. All major key ii-V-I progressions are diatonic. Notice also in Example 6 that the chords of a ii-V-I progression are consecutive in the circle of 5ths.

Example 6

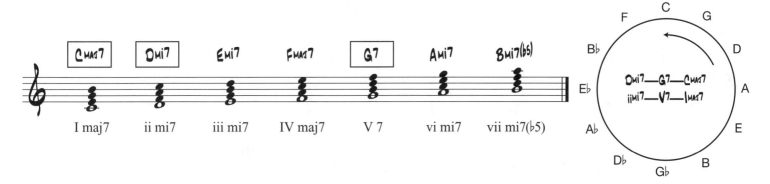

Most jazz standards contain as few as three to fifteen or more instances of the ii-V-I (or ii-V or I-vi-ii-V-I), so it is essential for every musician to have a solid understanding of this chord progression in all major and minor keys. You need to become good friends with this progression!

PATTERN P1 MAJOR

There are four specific ii-V-I voicing patterns you'll be playing in this book, Patterns P1, P2, P3 and P4. Each pattern relates to its corresponding voicing: Pattern P1 begins with Voicing P1 (5th on top), Pattern P2 begins with Voicing P2 (3rd on top), Pattern P3 begins with Voicing P3 (9th on top) and Pattern P4 begins with Voicing P4 (7th on top).

Example 7 illustrates ii-V-I Pattern P1 Major. In this pattern, Voicing P1 is used for the ii and I chords, and Voicing P3 (in four-note configuration) is used for the V7 chord. Notice that the chord symbol G9 is used for Voicing C to indicate a G dominant 7th chord with an added 9th.

Example 7

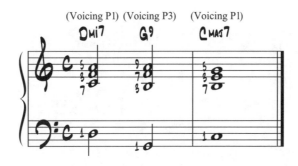

Exercise 15 features ii-V-I Pattern P1 Major for practice in all keys. Practice the patterns repeatedly until they become automatic. The idea is to develop muscle memory: your hands should remember what these chord shapes *feel* like. Your goal is to be able to play them perfectly at ♩=96. Though the exercises are written out in all keys, I strongly suggest playing the chords without reading them after your first few practice sessions.

PLAY **Exercise 15**

Once you've mastered Pattern P1 Major in all keys, you're ready to apply it to a song. To play a song will require a basic analysis of the song's chord progression. The name of the game is to locate the ii-V-I or partial (ii-V) progressions. As you approach most jazz standards, you will find that they move through at least several episodes of ii-V-I or ii-V in different key centers. When you locate these progressions, *mark them with an overhead bracket* and label their key center. Notice that Example 8 contains three complete ii-V-I progressions, each in a different key.

STUDY **Example 8**

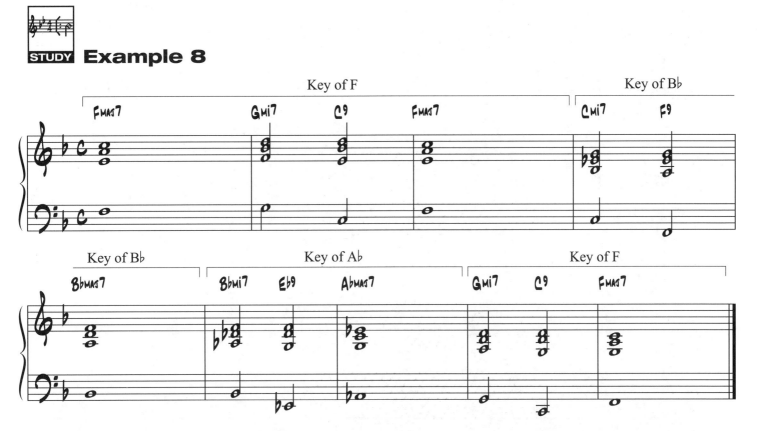

Bracketing the complete or partial ii-V-I chord progressions will help you quickly identify where you can use Pattern P1 in songs. For chords that are not part of the ii-V-I progression, omit brackets and simply play Voicing P1.

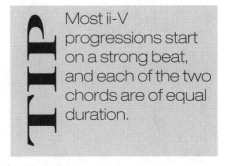

Most ii-V progressions start on a strong beat, and each of the two chords are of equal duration.

Play the chord changes to the first half of a jazz standard song in Exercise 16. (The melody is provided for your reference only.) This exercise uses voicings from ii-V-I Pattern P1 Major. The complete or partial ii-V-I progressions have been bracketed for easy identification. For chords that are not part of a ii-V or ii-V-I progression, Voicing P1 is used.

 **Exercise 16**
"Emily"

 **Track 1**

Music by JOHNNY MANDEL
Words by JOHNNY MERCER

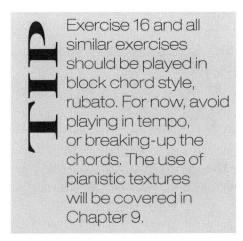

TIP Exercise 16 and all similar exercises should be played in block chord style, rubato. For now, avoid playing in tempo, or breaking-up the chords. The use of pianistic textures will be covered in Chapter 9.

VOICING P1 (MINOR SEVENTH, FLAT FIVE CHORDS)

The minor 7th, ♭5 chord type is prolific in all minor key songs, and also fairly common in major key songs. Example 9 illustrates Voicing P1 applied to a Cmi7♭5 chord. Note that the ♭5th is the top note of the voicing.

 **Example 9**

Exercise 17 takes Voicing P1 through all keys with minor 7th, ♭5 chords. Your goal is to be able to play them perfectly at ♩=80. Play them without reading after your first few practice sessions.

 **Exercise 17**
Minor Seventh, Flat Five Chords

PATTERN P1 MINOR

In minor keys, the chords of the ii-V-I progression are *not* diatonic; they are derived from more than one minor scale. However, the root movement and *chord function* is exactly the same as in the related major key progression. Chord function is a reference to the harmonic role of a given chord within a progression. For example in the key of C, a Dmi7 chord functions as the ii-7 chord. However, in the key of F, a Dmi7 chord functions as the vi-7 chord.

Example 10 illustrates ii-V-I Pattern P1 Minor. This pattern is very similar to ii-V-I Pattern P1 Major, though a few notes are adjusted to accommodate the minor key. Notice in this example that the V7 chord contains a ♭9th. A raised or lowered extension is referred to as an *altered note*. (More about altered notes in Chapter 6, pg. 66.)

 Example 10

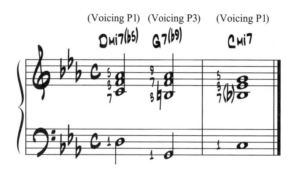

Exercise 18

Exercise 18 features ii-V-I Pattern P1 Minor for practice in all keys. Practice the patterns repeatedly until they become automatic. Your goal is to be able to play them perfectly at ♩=96.

Now apply ii-V-I Pattern P1 Minor to a tune. Notice in Exercise 19 that the complete or partial ii-V-I progressions are bracketed for easy identification. For chords that are not part of a ii-V or ii-V-I progression, Voicing P1 is used.

Exercise 19

"You'd Be So Nice To Come Home To"

Words and Music by COLE PORTER

Additional Practice:

Apply Pattern P1 to a jazz tune of your choice. For any chords that don't fall within the ii-V or ii-V-I pattern, play Voicing P1. Good song choices include "Autumn Leaves," "Bluesette," "Misty," and "What is This Thing Called Love." Remember that you first will need to do a brief chord progression analysis and bracket the ii-V or ii-V-I progressions.

TIP

At this stage of the game, your hands must frequently lift and relocate to different positions at the piano. This is only temporary. In Chapter 4 you'll learn how to combine patterns to connect the chords more smoothly.

THE DISTRIBUTION OF NOTES

The voicings in this chapter and throughout the remainder of **The Essentials** section are designed to be played with three notes in the right hand and only the bass note in the left (3+1). Though professional jazz pianists normally use an even distribution of notes between the two hands, the 3 + 1 distribution was chosen for the following reasons:

- By playing only the root of the chord in the left hand the chord is more readily visualized and understood.

- Adapting to rhythmic styles of playing will be a breeze since that process involves playing single note bass lines in the left hand and rhythmic chords in the right. (For more info about rhythmic styles, see *Chapter 5*.)

Be aware that when you develop the skills to play open voicings in a more pianistic way in the **Above and Beyond** section, voicings will have a distribution of two or more notes in the left hand and two or more in the right. Optionally, you can get a jump on things now by practicing the voicings in Chapters 2-5 two ways: with 3 notes in the right hand/one in the left, then also with 2 notes in the left hand and 2 in the right. This variation in your practice is not essential, but you may find it helpful for exercises down the road.

Chapter 3 Position #2 (P2)

> **GOAL:** Study and practice Voicing P2 and its related chord progression pattern, Pattern P2. Patterns P1 and P2 are the basis for exercises you'll play throughout the remainder of section I, **The Essentials**. Learn them well!

VOICING P2 (MAJOR, DOMINANT AND MINOR SEVENTH CHORDS)

Increasing your repertoire of voicings will provide greater interest and variety in your playing and allow you to connect the chords with smoother *voice leading*. Voice leading refers to the linear continuity between all voices, or notes of a chord, when moving from one chord to another.

The notes in Voicing P2 are (from the bottom up) the root, 5th, 7th (or the 6th), and 3rd of any chord. Example 11 illustrates Voicing P2 applied to major, dominant and minor 7th chords. Note that the 3rd is the top note of the voicing.

STUDY Example 11

Exercises 20-22 take Voicing P2 through all keys with major, dominant and minor 7th chords. Your goal is to be able to play them perfectly at ♩=80. As always, play the chords without reading them after your first few practice sessions.

Exercise 20
Major Seventh Chords

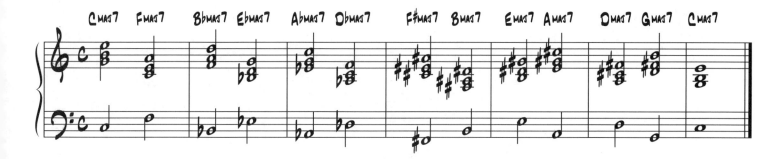

Exercise 21
Dominant Seventh Chords

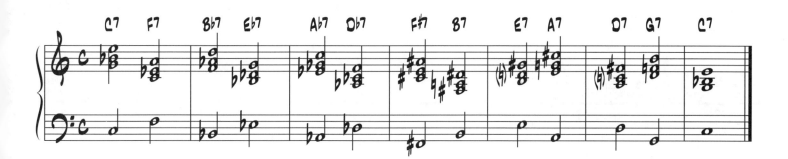

Exercise 22
Minor Seventh Chords

PATTERN P2 MAJOR

Example 12 illustrates ii-V-I Pattern P2 Major. In this pattern, Voicing P2 is used for the ii and I chords, and Voicing P4 (in four-note configuration) is used for the V7 chord. (You'll work more with Voicing P4 in five-note configuration in Chapter 7.) As with Pattern P1, the chord symbol G9 is used to indicate a G dominant 7th chord with an added 9th.

STUDY **Example 12**

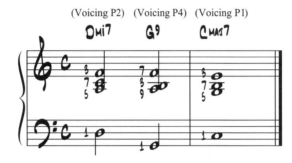

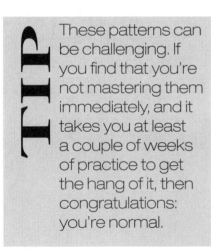

These patterns can be challenging. If you find that you're not mastering them immediately, and it takes you at least a couple of weeks of practice to get the hang of it, then congratulations: you're normal.

Exercise 23

Exercise 23 features ii-V-I Pattern P2 Major for practice in all keys. Practice the patterns repeatedly until they become automatic. Your goal is to be able to play them perfectly at ♩=96.

Now apply the ii-V-I Pattern P2 Major to a tune. Notice in Exercise 24 that the complete or partial ii-V-I progressions are bracketed for easy identification. For chords that are not part of a ii-V or ii-V-I progression, Voicing P2 is used.

Exercise 24
"Emily"

LISTEN Track 2

Music by JOHNNY MANDEL
Words by JOHNNY MERCER

VOICING P2 (MINOR SEVENTH, FLAT FIVE CHORDS)

Example 13 illustrates Voicing P2 applied to a Cmi7♭5 chord. Note that the ♭3rd is the top note of the voicing.

 STUDY **Example 13**

Exercise 25 takes Voicing P2 through all keys with minor 7th, ♭5 chords. Your goal is to be able to play them perfectly at ♩=96.

> **TIP**
> Just a reminder, for this and all short exercises that progress through the circle of 5ths:
>
> 1. Start in a different key each day to ensure fluency in all of the keys.
>
> 2. Play the chords without reading them after your first few practice sessions.

PLAY **Exercise 25**
Minor Seventh, Flat Five Chords

PATTERN P2 MINOR

Example 14 illustrates ii-V-I Pattern P2 Minor. This pattern is very similar to ii-V-I Pattern P2 Major though a few notes are adjusted to accommodate the minor key. Notice that just as in Pattern P1 Minor, the ♭5th of the iimi7♭5 chord (A♭) is the same note as the flat 9th of the V7(♭9) chord.

 STUDY **Example 14**

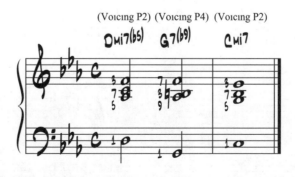

Exercise 26 features ii-V-I Pattern P2 Minor for practice in all major keys. Your goal is to be able to play them perfectly at ♩=96.

PLAY Exercise 26

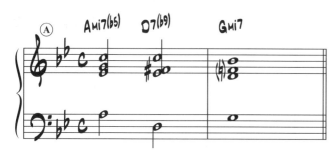

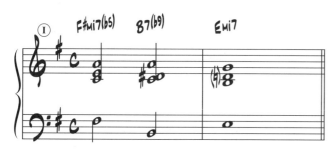

Now apply the ii-V-I Pattern P2 Minor to a tune. Notice in Exercise 27 that the complete or partial ii-V-I progressions are bracketed for easy identification. For chords that are not part of a ii-V or ii-V-I progression, Voicing P2 is used.

Exercise 27
"You'd Be So Nice To Come Home To"

Words and Music by COLE PORTER

  **Track 2**

Additional Practice:

Apply Pattern P2 to a jazz tune of your choice. For any chords that don't fall within the ii-V or ii-V-I pattern, play Voicing P2. Good song choices include "Autumn Leaves," "Bluesette," "Misty," and "What is This Thing Called Love." Remember that you first will need to do a brief chord progression analysis and bracket the ii-V or ii-V-I progressions.

Chapter  Applying the Patterns

CONNECTING THE DOTS

Using a combination of Position #1 (P1) and Position #2 (P2) within a song and shifting between these positions will allow your playing to sound more smooth and connected. Occasional repositioning of the hands will be necessary in any song, but the goal is to minimize this as much as possible. Switch octaves as needed to keep chords around the middle to mid-low register of the piano. Use your ears: if a voicing sounds muddy, it's too low!

Example 15 illustrates the approximate high and low range limits for your reference.

 Example 15

Notice that Example 16 begins in Position #2 and quickly shifts to Position #1, yet the hands move very little from their original location at the piano. This is an example of good voicing leading.

 Example 16

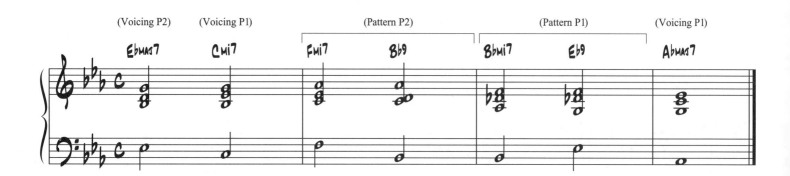

Example 17 illustrates a different version of the same progression used in Example 16, this time starting with Position #1. Note that again by mixing and matching Positions #1 and #2, the chords are connected smoothly with minimal repositioning of the hands.

Example 17

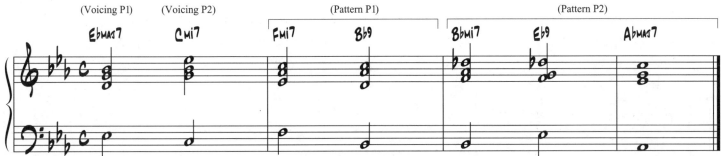

Exercise 28 "Emily"

Play Exercises 28 and 29, each of which utilize a mixture of Voicings and Patterns P1 and P2. See Exercises 16 and 19 (pgs. 26, 30) for references to the melody of each song.

LISTEN **Track 3**

Music by JOHNNY MANDEL
Words by JOHNNY MERCER

Exercise 29
"You'd Be So Nice To Come Home To"

LISTEN Track 3

Music by JOHNNY MANDEL
Words by JOHNNY MERCER

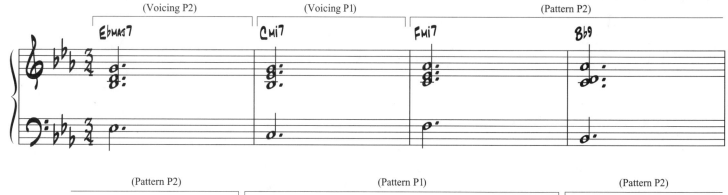

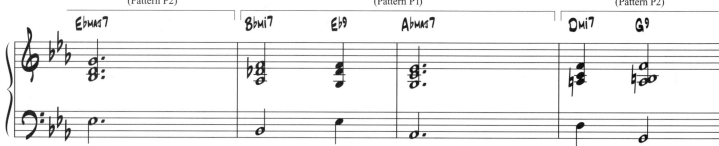

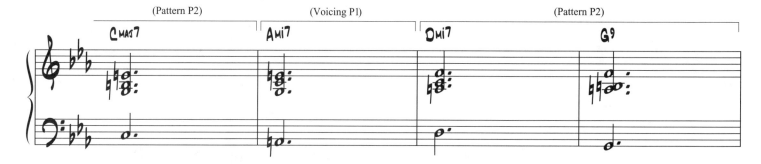

Additional Practice:

Play through Etudes 1 and 2 in Appendix I and listen to the corresponding CD Tracks 11 and 12. Also, using a song of your choice, mix and match Positions #1 and #2. Try to make the voice leading as smooth as possible. Good song choices include "Autumn Leaves," "Bluesette," "Misty," and "What is This Thing Called Love."

THE NATURE OF CHORD PROGRESSIONS

Playing jazz piano would be relatively simple if all chord progressions fell neatly into one of our ii-V-I, ii-V, or I-vi-ii-V-I patterns with little or no variation. But, most tunes venture out of these harmonic patterns often, and thankfully so because otherwise they would become predictable and boring!

Navigating successfully through the harmonic idiosyncrasies of jazz standards requires a deeper look into how the songs are constructed. The following is an overview of the harmonic tendency of most standard tunes.

1. A key center is established in the beginning.

2. Then a departure to one or more temporary key centers. Songs often move through a number of different key centers.

3. Finally, a return to the original key center (or sometimes a different, final key center) via movement in the circle of 5ths.

Example 18 illustrates the harmonic construction of a typical jazz standard progression. The slashes within the stave represent beats of the measure.

STUDY **Example 18**

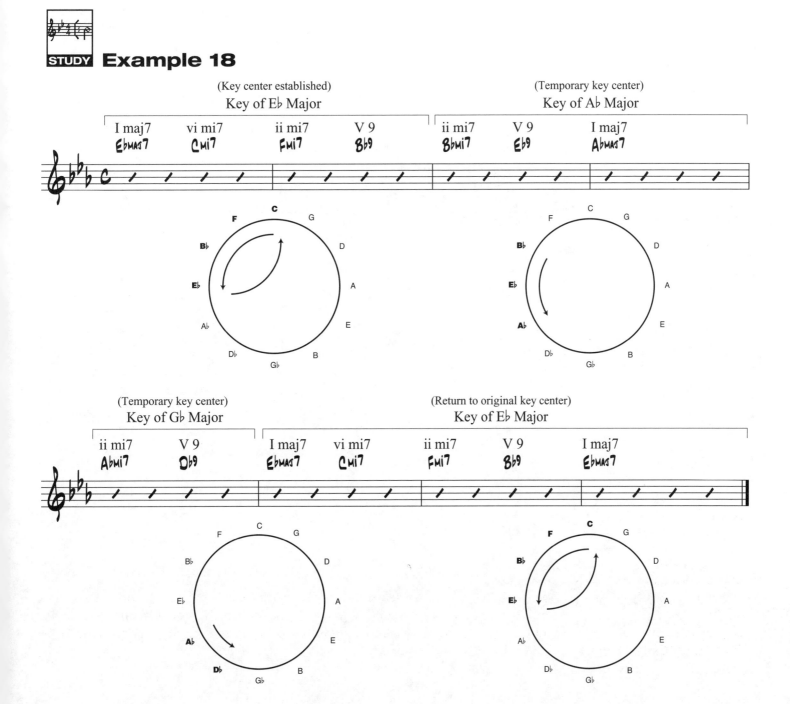

Take a look at the harmonic analysis as illustrated in Example 19. This progression moves through brief episodes in several different key centers. Notice that the Cmi7 chord functions in two keys as a *pivot chord*. Pivot chords serve as a link between one key center with the next, helping to smooth the transition during a harmonic modulation.

STUDY **Example 19**

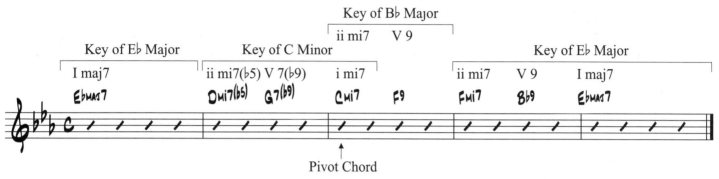

Jazz standards are generally comprised of episodes of movement in different key centers. Most tunes move through anywhere from three to eight keys. Get used to this idea and with a little practice, you'll be able to spot the key center shifts easily.

FAQ: WHAT DO I DO IF....

The harmonic patterns you've already studied (ii-V-I, ii-V, and I-vi-ii-V-I) will apply to about 75 percent of all jazz standard chord progressions. But, what about the other 25 percent? As a well-rounded pianist you need to be able to recognize new, unfamiliar progressions and have the skills to accommodate them in your playing. In this section you'll study variations in otherwise familiar patterns and other common harmonic occurrences you're likely to encounter.

WHAT DO I DO IF...

I see what looks like a complete or partial I-vi-ii-V-I progression, but one or more of the chord *types* (such as major 7th or dominant 7th) is not what it's expected to be in the context of the progression?

ANSWER:

It's common for ii-V, ii-V-I or I-vi-ii-V-I patterns to be modified by use of dominant 7th chords in place of the vi and the ii. Examples can be found in numerous tunes including "It's Only A Paper Moon," "My Ship, " Our Love is Here To Stay," and "Take the A Train." Example 20 illustrates a dominant 7th chord in place of the vi mi7 chord in the song, "Secret Love."

Example 20
"Secret Love"

Words by PAUL FRANCIS WEBSTER
Music by SAMMY FAIN

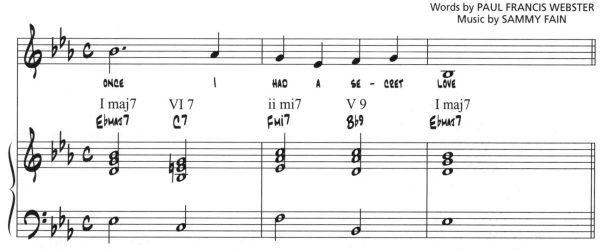

The VI7 chord illustrated in Example 20 is often referred to as a *secondary dominant*. A secondary dominant is simply a dominant 7th chord a perfect fifth above the chord it's progressing to, regardless of the key of the song. Secondary dominants function as the temporary V7 of the chord they're approaching. Observe the alternate style of Roman numerals used to label the secondary dominants in Example 21.

Example 21
"Secret Love"

Words by PAUL FRANCIS WEBSTER
Music by SAMMY FAIN

WHAT DO I DO IF…

I see what looks like a I-vi-ii-V-I progression, but one of the chords seem to be wrong; it's out of place in the context of this pattern?

ANSWER:

Chances are that the out of place chord is functioning as a substitute chord. Two common types of substitutions within the I-vi-ii-V-I progression are described below. When playing the progressions in each of the following cases, simply use Patterns P1 or P2 as a basis, and use Voicing P1 or P2 for the chord in question.

    1. A diminished 7th chord built on the flat 3rd scale degree in place of the vi chord.

Examples can be found in the following tunes: "I've Got A Crush on You," "How About You," "Nevertheless," and "On the Street Where You Live." Example 22 illustrates a diminished 7th chord built on the flat 3rd scale degree in the song, "Embraceable You."

STUDY Example 22 "Embraceable You"

Music and Lyrics by
GEORGE GERSHWIN and IRA GERSHWIN

© 1930 (Renewed) WB MUSIC CORP.
All Rights Reserved

    2. A diminished 7th chord built on the raised 1st scale degree may be found in place of the vi chord.

Examples can be found in numerous tunes including the following: "Bewitched," "You Make Me Feel So Young," "Takin' A Chance on Love," "Lullaby of Broadway." Example 23 illustrates a diminished 7th chord built on the raised 1st scale degree in the song, "Ain't Misbehavin."

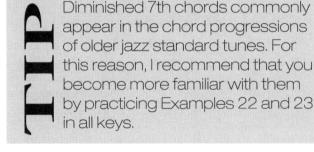

TIP — Diminished 7th chords commonly appear in the chord progressions of older jazz standard tunes. For this reason, I recommend that you become more familiar with them by practicing Examples 22 and 23 in all keys.

STUDY Example 23 "Ain't Misbehavin'"

Music by THOMAS "FATS" WALLER and HARRY BROOKS
Words by ANDY RAZAF

© 1929 (Renewed) EMI MILLS MUSIC INC., CHAPPELL & CO., INC. and RAZAF MUSIC CO.
All Rights Reserved

WHAT DO I DO IF...

there are numbers or other information attached to the chord symbols, such as a "13," "#11," and/or "♭5?"

ANSWER:

Chords often have extensions such as 9ths, 11ths and 13ths, or chord tone alterations such as #5 or ♭5 associated with chord symbols. (See Chapter 6 for a detailed description of color notes.) In some cases, the indicated notes are essential, and in other cases, they are not. Here's the rule of thumb: if the chord symbol dictates a certain color note, look at the song's melody. If that color note appears in the melody, and your usual chord voicing would otherwise clash with it, then you should incorporate the note into your voicing. If your usual voicing would not clash with a color note in the melody, then its inclusion is optional. Notice in Example 24 that the ♭9 on the C7(♭9) chord is optional, but the #9 on the B♭7(#9) is not.

Example 24
STUDY "Since I Fell For You"

Words and Music by BUDDY JOHNSON

(♭9 optional)   (#9 not optional)

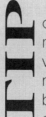

TIP

Take care that the top notes of your chord voicings don't clash with the melody. If the top note of a voicing is within a half step of a held note in the melody, it will not sound good! Adjust by altering the top note or using a different voicing.

WHAT DO I DO IF…
there's a chord symbol I don't recognize, like E♭7/F?

ANSWER:

Generally, when you see a chord symbol that you don't recognize, refer to Diagram 6 in Appendix II: Chord Symbols and Color Notes Chart, pg. 125. In this particular example, you would play an E♭ dominant 7th chord over the bass note, F as illustrated in Example 25. This is commonly referred to as a *slash chord*. A slash chord is a chord played over a single bass note that is different than the root of that chord.

Example 25
"A Time for Love"

Music by JOHNNY MANDEL
Words by PAUL FRANCIS WEBSTER

WHAT DO I DO IF…

I'm sure I'm playing the correct chord voicings but the song still doesn't sound good?

ANSWER:

First, *how* sure are you that the notes you're playing are completely correct? One slip of the finger to a wrong note can make a world of difference. Before anything else, I recommend first triple checking the notes in your voicing! Secondly, the problem could be that the chord changes you're using are faulty. Some of the older published fake books contain chord progressions that are not written in a style that's conducive to jazz playing, or are just plain wrong. This is why it's important that you have a modern fake book with correct chord changes, such as *Just Standards Real Book*, (Alfred Publishing), *Just Jazz Real Book*, (Alfred Publishing), or *The Standards Real Book* (Sher Music Company). See more about faulty chord symbols in "Melodic Troublemakers," Chapter 10, pg. 107.

Additional Practice:

Practice playing jazz standards with harmonic episodes that depart from the familiar ii-V-I, ii-V, or I-vi-ii-V-I progressions. (There are many!) Good choices include any of the songs mentioned in the "FAQ: What Do I Do If…" section.

PLAYING SONGS IN OTHER KEYS

Ever wonder how experienced pianists and guitarists can remember so many songs and be able to play them in any key? This skill is actually not as mysterious as it seems. Players who can readily transpose songs to other keys are thinking of the song's shifting chord progression patterns as a *formula*.

For example, the formula for the tune, "Emily" begins with Imaj7-vi7-ii7-V7-Imaj7 in the song's actual key, E♭. (This should now seem to you like an easy formula to plug into any key!) After the first five bars of "Emily" in E♭, the song temporarily shifts to the key of A♭ (the *IV* chord of the *original key*) via a ii-7-V7-Imaj7 progression. Then, it shifts to the key of C (the *VI* chord of the *original key*) via another ii-7-V7-Imaj7 progression. The formula for the first 8 bars of "Emily" is summarized in Example 26.

 STUDY ## Example 26

1. Imaj7-vi7-ii7-V7-Imaj7 in the song's key [E♭]

2. ii-7-V7-Imaj7 in the key of the IV chord [A♭]

3. ii-7-V7-Imaj7 in the key of the VI chord [C]

Music by JOHNNY MANDEL
Words by JOHNNY MERCER

Once the formula for any song has been identified, it is then relatively easy to apply it to any key. Example 27 illustrates the chord changes of "Emily" in the key of C.

 STUDY ## Example 27

Music by JOHNNY MANDEL
Words by JOHNNY MERCER

Try playing the first eight bars of "Emily" in several different keys. This extra practice is not essential, but you may find it a valuable exercise, and easier than you think!

Chapter 5 Rhythmic Styles

> **GOAL:** Apply Patterns P1 and P2 to rhythmic styles such as swing, bossa nova and so on. Develop good left hand/right hand rhythmic coordination while maintaining a strong sense of steady time.

Now that you've mastered the voicing patterns from the preceding chapters, you're ready, and probably anxious to begin playing in rhythm. Be aware that there's still a lot to learn about expanding your repertoire of voicings and playing pianistically in rubato. You'll continue on that path in the next section, **Above and Beyond**. In the meantime, dust off that metronome!

The coordination required for the right hand to play a different rhythm than the left while maintaining steady time can be a challenge. With this in mind, short practice patterns will be used to help you get the feel of the rhythms and to train your hands to play independently. In rhythmic playing your left hand is analogous to the bass player, and therefore should function similarly to the bass player in terms of maintaining steady tempo and drive.

SWING

A mastery of swing feel is vital for any jazz musician. Swing is primarily a 4/4 feel although it can also be played in other meters. The essence of swing feel is the underlying feeling of eighth-note triplets and accents on beats 2 and 4. The eighth-note triplet feel is most apparent at a slow tempo, but when the tempo increases it becomes less apparent. Example 28 illustrates how written eighth notes are *interpreted* as triplets in swing feel.

STUDY Example 28

   interpreted as:

When playing piano is a swing style, the left hand will play a *walking bass line*, exactly the same way the bass player plays in an instrumental jazz group. A walking bass line is made up primarily of quarter notes, with the root of the chord played on the first beat of every new chord and arpeggiated or scalar passing notes in between. You'll *comp* in your right hand—play rootless chord voicings in a rhythmic way. Comping is short for accompanying or complementing.

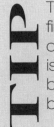
To create a solid swing feel, you will first need to develop a great sense of time. Practicing with a metronome is essential. Try changing the click to beats 2 and 4 to help internalize the off beat syncopation.

WALKING BASS LINES

Here's a step-by-step guide on how to construct a walking bass line.

1. Play the root of the chord when the chord changes, usually on beats 1 or 3. For now, fill in the other beats with repeated quarter notes.

Example 29

2. Connect the chords using a combination of diatonic stepwise motion and arpeggiated notes.

Example 30

3. Add occasional chromatic passing notes, making sure that they lead to a chord tone.

Example 31

4. Finally, add a little rhythmic variation.

Example 32

RHYTHMIC PATTERNS FOR COMPING IN SWING

There are common rhythmic patterns that recur often in the swing style. These familiar rhythms are the basis for what you'll use in your right hand comping. Example 33 illustrates examples of typical swing rhythms.

STUDY Example 33

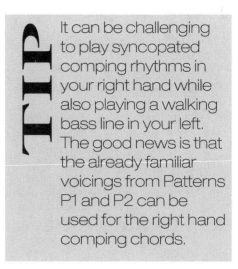

Play the short patterns in Exercise 30, starting with the left hand bass lines only. Then, practice only the right hand comping parts. Finally, put the two together and use a metronome at every stage of the game! Your goal is to be able to play them perfectly at ♩ = 104, but you may want to start slower and work up to that tempo. Use right hand Voicings P1 and P2 interchangeably as you wish.

 **Exercise 30**

TIP
Optionally, play each of the patterns in Exercise 30 in at least two other keys. This extra practice is not essential, but it would be helpful in solidifying your expertise in this style.

SWING "2" FEEL

A swing "2" feel differs from the "4" feel described above in that each measure feels like it has two beats per measure and there is no walking bass line. Example 34 illustrates that the majority of bass notes in a "2" feel are half notes, or dotted eighth/eighth note pairs with occasional passing notes.

 **STUDY** **Example 34**

The "2" feel has a much lighter rhythmic feeling than "4" feel, and is often used at the beginning of jazz standards during the first section or the entire first *chorus* of the song. The term chorus is commonly used by jazz musicians to indicate one time thru the form of the song. In typical jazz performance practice, after the "2" feel, the bass player will go into "4" (characterized by a walking bass line,) giving the music more drive and sense of forward motion.

Play the short patterns in Exercise 31. You may want to begin by playing the left hand bass lines only as you did in Exercise 30. I recommend you also play each exercise in at least two other keys. Your goal is to be able to play them perfectly at ♩ = 104. Feel free to use voicings P1 and P2 interchangeably.

PLAY **Exercise 31**

Now you'll apply a combination of walking ("4" feel) and "2" feel bass lines with comp chords to a jazz standard. The song's melody is an important consideration when devising your right hand comping rhythms. The goal is to complement and support the melody without getting in its way rhythmically. Comping rhythms should either coincide exactly with the natural accents in the melody, or they should be static when the melody is active, filling in the holes when the melody is at rest.

Play Exercise 32, making every effort to maintain steady tempo and sense of drive in the left hand as a bass player would. The melody is provided for reference only. Notice that the song alternates between "2" and "4" feel. Your goal should be to play it perfectly at the indicated metronome marking.

Exercise 32
"East of the Sun"

LISTEN Track 4

Words and Music by BROOKS BOWMAN

Additional Practice:

Play through Etudes 3 and 4 in Appendix I and listen to the corresponding CD Tracks 13 and 14. (Always practice with a metronome in rhythmic styles.) Also, using a song of your choice, write a bass line with the first half in "2" feel, then a walking bass line starting at the second half. Play it along with improvised right hand comping. Once you've practiced writing out "2" and "4" feel bass lines on several tunes, you can begin improvising them on the fly. Good song choices include "All of Me," "Fly Me To the Moon," "I Can't Give You Anything But Love," and "You'd Be So Nice to Come Home To."

BOSSA NOVA

Bossa nova is a Brazilian rhythmic style that has a *straight-eighth* feel, as opposed to the swing eighths used in swing feel. Straight-eighths or even-eighths are simply eighth notes that are played with an even subdivision, not swung. Example 35 illustrates the basic bass line pattern for a bossa.

 STUDY **Example 35**

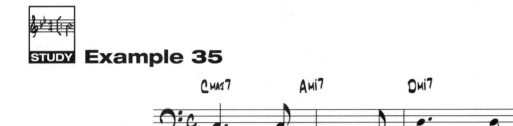

The right hand comping rhythms are usually quite syncopated in the bossa nova style. Example 36 illustrates a typical comping pattern and two variations.

STUDY **Example 36**

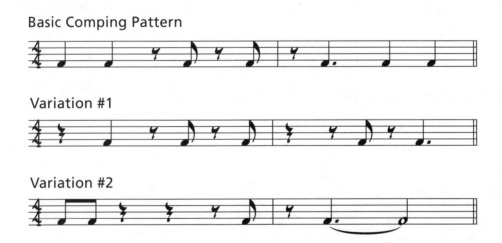

For the chord progression patterns in Exercise 33, first play the bass lines only, then the right hand chords only. Finally, put the two together and as always, use a metronome. I recommend you play each exercise in at least two other keys. Your goal should be to play it perfectly at ♩ = 104. Use right hand Voicings P1 and P2 interchangeably as you wish. Notice how the bass pattern changes slightly when there are two chords per bar rather than one. Also, you'll see that in each example, the last chord of the first measure is an *anticipation* of the chord in the second measure.

Exercise 33

Now apply the bossa nova style to a song in Exercise 34. The melody is provided for your reference only. You may again find it helpful to practice the left hand and right hands separately before putting them together. (Don't forget to use that metronome!)

Exercise 34
"Gentle Rain"

LISTEN Track 5

By LUIZ BONFA

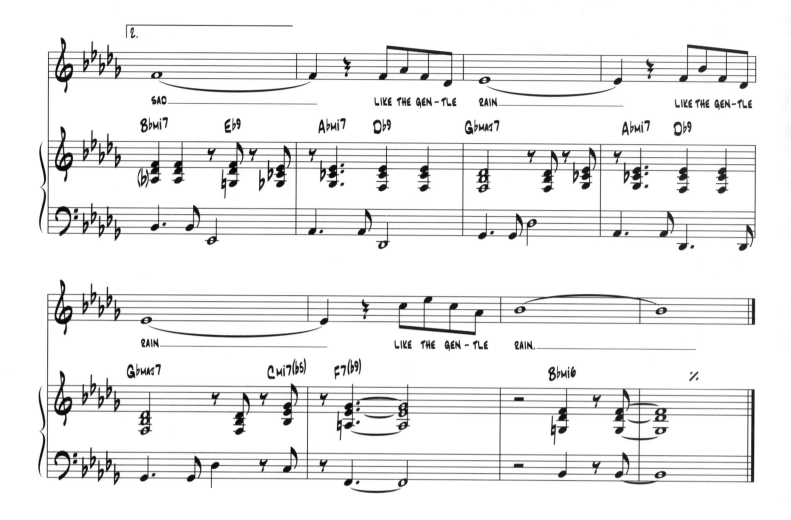

Additional Practice:

Play through Etude 5 in Appendix I and listen to the corresponding CD Track 15. Also, experiment with playing other songs of your choice in the bossa style. Good song choices include "Desafinado," "Girl From Ipanema," "Meditation" and "How Insensitive."

TIP Rhythmic simplicity is best. Remember that your right hand comping rhythms should complement the song's melody, not detract from it. Sometimes less is better!

ADDITIONAL RHYTHMIC STYLES

There are numerous other rhythmic styles in jazz besides swing and bossa nova. Although this publication cannot cover them all, see descriptions and examples of a few of the more common styles below. I recommend that you practice each of the following short examples in at least several keys, with a metronome.

JAZZ WALTZ

As the name implies, *jazz waltz* is in 3/4 meter. However, it differs from a traditional waltz in that the eighth notes are swing eighths (♪♪ = ♪♪ or ♪♪) just like in swing feel. The triplet (swing) eighths give this style its characteristic *lilt*. Jazz waltz can be played two ways, first, with a feeling of 1 beat per measure as in Exercise 35.

 Exercise 35

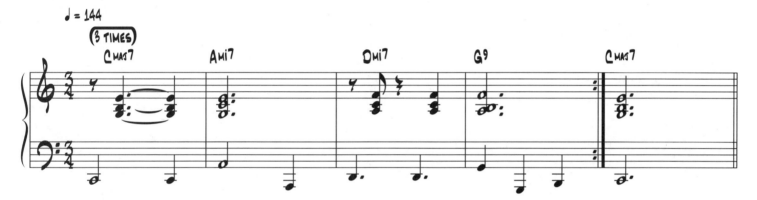

Jazz waltz can also be played with a feeling of 3 beats per measure as in Exercise 36. Notice the walking bass line.

 Exercise 36

Jazz waltz is similar to swing "2" and "4" feels in that it is lighter and more buoyant when played in "1," and more driving when in "3." Good song choices for additional practice of jazz waltz include "Bluesette," "Falling in Love With Love" and "Someday My Prince Will Come."

SAMBA

Samba is another style from Brazil and very similar to bossa nova, though usually faster. It differs from bossa nova in that it is in "2:" each measure feels like it has two beats per measure, not four. As you play Exercise 37, you will notice the bass line consists primarily of half notes.

Exercise 37

Good song choices for additional practice of Samba include "Chega De Saudade" (No More Blues), "One Note Samba," and "So Nice" (Summer Samba).

BALLAD TEMPO

The *jazz ballad* is one of the trickiest rhythmic styles for a solo pianist. It can be characterized as having a slow, steady feeling of four beats per measure, usually with a slight underlying eighth note triplet feeling. The challenge in playing this style is to propel the song forward in a very steady but slow tempo while not over playing. A good general approach to playing ballad tempo is to play half note chords on beats one and three, and very sparse melodic or chordal passing notes on the weak beats (2 and 4) to help propel the rhythm. (For more about passing notes, see Chapter 9, pg. 97.) Practice the basic principles of jazz ballad style in Exercise 38.

Exercise 38

For more practice at ballad tempo, play through Etude 6 in Appendix I and listen to the corresponding CD Track 16. (To effectively illustrate ballad tempo playing, Etude 6 incorporates concepts from Chapters 6– 9 including four and five-note open and closed voicings, color notes, pianistic texture, and Voicings P3 and P4.) Also, play through other songs of your choice in the ballad style. Good song choices include "Lover Man," "Stormy Weather" and "You Don't Know What Love Is."

CHECK YOUR PROGRESS

Congratulations on the progress you've made so far! At this point you should be well prepared to play basic jazz piano.

Before moving on, this a good time to take inventory of how you are doing. Here are a few questions to consider:

1. Can you open a fake book, play the chord changes of a song in a musical way with 90 percent accuracy, and at a reasonable tempo?

2. Are you comfortable with Patterns P1 and P2, being able to mix and match them with smooth voice leading when applied to a song?

3. Do you have a basic understanding of the harmonic structure of jazz standards, and can you easily spot the ii-V, ii-V-I, and I-vi-ii-V-I progressions within tunes?

4. Can you play any song comfortably in a medium swing feel or bossa?

Depending on how you answered the above questions, you should now determine whether it's best to

1. Continue to the next group of chapters: **Above and Beyond**.

2. Go back and review certain material, spending more practice time with certain exercises.

3. Apply what you're learned to more songs of your choice before starting on new material.

Whenever you are certain you're fully prepared and ready to move forward, the following chapters will take you to another musical level and give you creative tools for playing in a more interesting and pianistic way.

Chapter

6 Expanding Your Palette

GOAL: Study color notes from a theoretical point of view and learn how they can be integrated into Patterns P1 and P2 through the use of five-note voicings. Color notes such as extensions and altered chord tones are a fundamental feature of jazz harmony.

COLOR NOTES

EXTENSIONS

Extensions are non-chord tones, specifically the 9th, 11th and 13th scale degrees, added to chords for interest. (You will recall that the 9th and the ♭9th have already been used in the dominant 7th chords of Patterns P1 and P2.) Extensions are derived from chords built in thirds that extend beyond the seventh scale degree as illustrated in Example 37.

 STUDY **Example 37**

TIP It's not necessary to assimilate the information in this section all at once! For now, simply read through the material to get a general overview.

Below is a description of each extension, including its character and typical use.

1. The *9th* is the same note as the 2nd scale degree. Use with any chord type. The 9th is by far the most commonly used color note so I recommend you get in the habit of adding a 9th to your chords whenever possible. On most chord voicings the 9th adds a pleasant, pretty quality. On minor 7th, ♭5 and diminished chords, it creates dissonance.

 Example 38

The 9th is always a whole step above the root of the chord, even if that note is not diatonic in the key. Example 39 illustrates a five-note voicing for the iimi9(♭5) chord in the key of C minor. (More about five-note voicings later in this chapter.)

 Example 39

2. The *11th* is the same note as the fourth scale degree. Use with minor family and diminished family chords. The 11th provides a warm, stable sound on minor family chords, but adds dissonance when used on a diminished chord.

 Example 40

3. The *13th* is the same note as the sixth scale degree. Use with major 7th, dominant 7th, and sparingly on minor 7th and minor/major 7th chords. Like the 9th, the 13th adds a pleasant, pretty quality to major and dominant 7th chords. When used on minor 7th chords, it adds a great deal of dissonance.

 Example 41

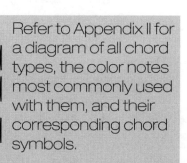
TIP Refer to Appendix II for a diagram of all chord types, the color notes most commonly used with them, and their corresponding chord symbols.

ALTERED NOTES

Altered Notes are chord tones or extensions that are raised or lowered by a half step: ♭9, #9, ♭5, #5, #11, ♭13. Altered notes are most often used with dominant 7th chords (though not exclusively,) and are more dissonant than unaltered notes such as 9ths and 13ths.

1. The *♭9th* is used with dominant 7th and dominant 7th sus chords. The ♭9th has a sympathetic, sad quality, and a strong tendency toward resolution down a half-step. Use of ♭9th on a dominant 7th chord creates a tendency for the chord to resolve down a 5th. For example, a G7(♭9) chord will most often progress to a C major or C minor chord.

 Example 42

2. The *#9th* is used with dominant 7th chords. The #9th is quite dissonant and is commonly used in blues and other blues based styles like R&B and gospel.

 Example 43

The indication, "alt" is often used in chord symbols to indicate the addition of one or more altered notes, at the discretion of the player (i.e., "C7alt"). In written music, altered notes frequently have enharmonic spellings. Notice in Example 44 that the #9th note is spelled as a ♭3rd.

 Example 44

3. The *#11th* is used with major family and dominant 7th chords. The #11th creates tension yet doesn't have the strong pull to resolve as with the ♭9th or ♭13th. The dominant 7th chord containing a 9th, #11th and 13th is commonly used at the end of a song as the final, dramatic held chord.

 Example 45

4. The *♭13th* is used with dominant 7th, diminished 7th, and sparingly on minor 7th, ♭5 chords. Like the ♭9th, this extension has a sympathetic and sad quality, and the same tendency toward resolution down a half step. Also, on a dominant 7th chord the ♭13th creates a tendency for the chord to resolve down a 5th. For example, a G7(♭13) chord will most often progress to a C major or C minor chord.

 Example 46

5. The *♭5th* is used with dominant 7th and major family chords. Note that although the ♭5th and ♯11th are the same note, theoretically they are used in slightly different ways: use of a ♭5th in a chord precludes the inclusion of a natural (unaltered) 5th, whereas a chord with the ♯11th may also contain a natural 5th. Most of the time in common practice however, if a ♯11th is used in a chord voicing, the 5th of the chord is omitted.

 Example 47

6. The *♯5th* is used with dominant 7th and sparingly on major and minor family chords. As with the ♭5th and ♯11th, the theoretical distinction between the ♯5th and ♭13th is this: use of a ♯5th precludes the inclusion of a natural 5th, whereas a ♭13th could possibly also contain a natural 5th. (Though as with the ♯11th, in common practice if a ♭13th is used in a chord voicing, the 5th is usually omitted.)

 Example 48

The ♯5th also commonly occurs as a passing note on both major and minor chords. You'll recognize the minor key example below from a very familiar spy movie theme.

 Example 49

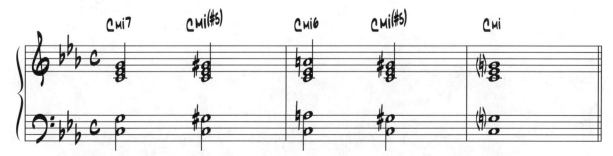

Diminished 7th chords are built entirely in minor thirds, making their intervallic structure symmetrical. The easiest way to think about adding extensions to diminished 7th chords is as follows: *you can add any note a whole step above any of the chord tones.* (The extensions technically are the 9th, 11th, ♭13th and major 7th notes, but you'll find them quicker by thinking of them the other way!) Example 50 illustrates each of the possible extensions for C°7.

STUDY **Example 50**

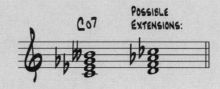

COMBINING EXTENSIONS AND ALTERED NOTES

It is possible to combine two or even three extensions or altered notes within a single chord. A general rule is that the more altered notes in the chord, the more dramatic impact the chord will have. For example, a natural 13th paired with a natural 9th will have a pleasant but sophisticated sound. However pairing a natural 13th with a ♭9th will create more tension with a bittersweet feeling. A 9th coupled with a ♯5th on a dominant 7th chord will result in the charming but dated sound associated with early twentieth-century popular songs. ("Shine On Harvest Moon," for example.) However an *altered* 9th joined with a ♯5th carries much more dramatic tension, and will have a more contemporary jazz sound. Have fun experimenting with the options!

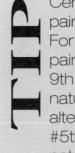

Certain color note pairings will clash. For example, avoid pairing an altered 9th paired with a natural 9th, or an altered 13th (or #5th) paired with a natural 13th.

FIVE-NOTE VOICINGS

Five-note voicings have a fuller sound and allow much more flexibility for the integration of color notes than four-note voicings. Numerous combinations of color notes are possible. The voicings in Patterns P1 and P2 can be modified to five-note voicings by simply adding an extra note to each chord. Example 51 illustrates Pattern P1 in a five-note configuration with extensions.

STUDY **Example 51**

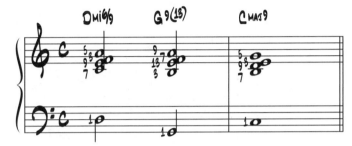

In minor ii-V-I progressions, the use of altered notes on the V7 chord is standard practice. Example 52 illustrates the use of both ♭9th and ♭13th on the G7 chord. Notice also in this example that the I chord is a minor 6th chord, another common occurrence in minor ii-V-I progressions.

STUDY **Example 52**

Play Patterns P1 Major and P1 Minor in Exercise 39. Play them as written, or vary the color notes as you wish. Your goal is to be able to play them perfectly at ♩ = 88. Notice that unlike the ii-V-I practice patterns from earlier chapters, Exercise 39 takes each pattern through the circle of 5ths. This will require your hands to lift and relocate for each exercise.

Exercise 39
Major

Minor

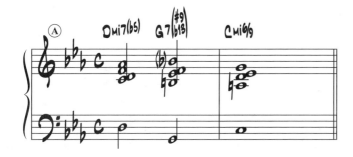

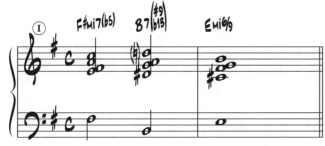

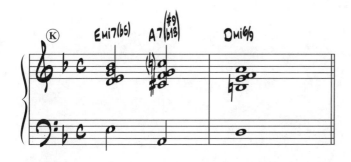

Altered notes can also be added to major key patterns with good effect. Example 53 illustrates Pattern P2 Major with a ♭9th and ♭5th on the V7 chord.

STUDY **Example 53**

Example 54 illustrates Pattern P2 Minor in five-note configuration. The 9th was omitted from the I and ii chords in this example because its addition would've resulted in a very dissonant half-step between the top two voices. However, the V7 chord contains both a ♭9th and ♭13th.

STUDY **Example 54**

Exercise 40
Major

Play Patterns P2 Major and P2 Minor as written in Exercise 40. Your goal is to be able to play them perfectly at ♩ = 88.

Ⓐ Dmi7 G7(♭9/♭5) Cmaj9

Ⓑ Gmi7 C7(♭9/♭5) Fmaj9

Ⓒ Cmi7 F7(♭9/♭5) B♭maj9

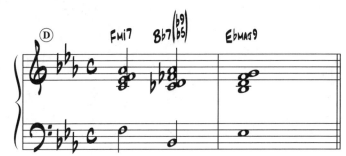

Ⓓ Fmi7 B♭7(♭9/♭5) E♭maj9

Ⓔ B♭mi7 E♭7(♭9/♭5) A♭maj9

Ⓕ E♭mi7 A♭7(♭9/♭5) D♭maj9

Ⓖ G♯mi7 C♯7(♭9/♭5) F♯maj9

Ⓗ C♯mi7 F♯7(♭9/♭5) Bmaj9

Ⓘ F♯mi7 B7(♭9/♭5) Emaj9

Ⓙ Bmi7 E7(♭9/♭5) Amaj9

Ⓚ Emi7 A7(♭9/♭5) Dmaj9

Ⓛ Ami7 D7(♭9/♭5) Gmaj9

🎹 Minor

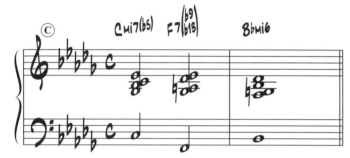

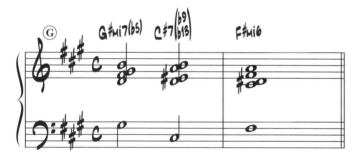

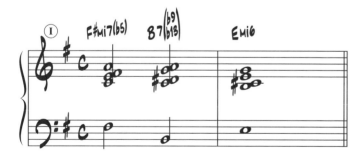

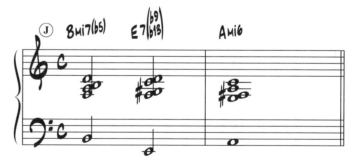

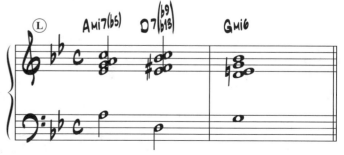

The song's melody is an important consideration when using color notes. Extensions or altered notes should always work harmoniously with the melody, never detracting from it. For example if the melody is on the 5th of a given chord, do not add a ♯11th or ♭13th to your chord voicing. Generally, avoid the interval of a half step between the top note of your voicing and the melody.

Now apply five-note voicings with color notes to the first half of a jazz standard song in Exercise 41. Notice that the voicing choices are a good complement to the melody.

 Exercise 41
"Shadow of Your Smile"

 **Track 6**

Music by JOHNNY MANDEL
Lyric by PAUL FRANCIS WEBSTER

TIP Remember, for short exercises written in all 12 keys, always play them without reading after your first couple of practice sessions.

Additional Practice:

Play through Etude 7 in Appendix I and listen to the corresponding CD Track 17. Also, experiment with adding color notes to Patterns P1 and P2 when playing through songs of your choice. Good song choices include "Alone Together," "Devil May Care," "Laura" and "On A Clear Day."

CHORD SYMBOL MADNESS

Unfortunately, there is currently no standardization for chord symbol nomenclature. Any chord type with color notes can be represented in quite a few different ways, and often is. If you are sometimes confused by certain chord symbols and what they are meant to indicate, you're not alone! When in doubt, refer to Appendix II which contains a comprehensive diagram of chord types and color note combinations, along with the chord symbols that could be used to represent them.

Chapter **7** Positions #3 (P3) and #4 (P4)

GOAL: Expand your repertoire of voicings with the study and practice of five-note Voicings and Patterns P3 and P4. Mix and match Voicings P1, P2, P3 and P4 for greater variety and better voice leading in your playing.

VOICING AND PATTERN P3

The notes of Voicing P3 in five-note configuration are (from the bottom up) the root, 3rd, 5th, 7th (or the 6th) and 9th. Example 55 illustrates Voicing P3 applied to major, dominant, minor, and minor 7th, ♭5 chords. Voicing P3 should already be very familiar to you because it was used in its four-note configuration for the V7 chord of Pattern P1. Note that the 9th is the top note of the voicing.

 Example 55

Example 56 illustrates ii-V-I Pattern P3 Major. Notice that the V7 chord in this pattern uses Voicing P1 in a five-note configuration, with the 13th substituting for the 5th. The V7 chord would also work well with altered notes such as the ♭9th and ♭13th in place of the 9th and 13th.

 Example 56

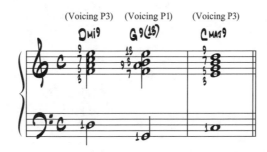

Pattern P3 Minor is illustrated in Example 57. Notice that the root of the chord is used for the top note of the iimi7(♭5) chord. Though the 9th would've also been an option, the root is considerably less dissonant, therefore, more commonly used.

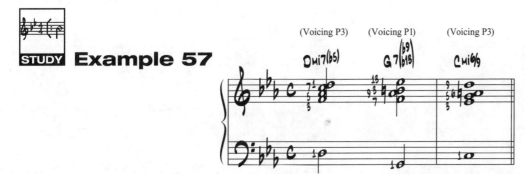 **Example 57**

Exercise 42
Major

Play Patterns P3 Major and P3 Minor as written in Exercise 42. Your goal is to be able to play them perfectly at ♩ = 88.

Minor

VOICING AND PATTERN P4

The notes in Voicing P4 in five-note configuration are (from the bottom up) the root, 9th, 3rd, 5th and 7th, (or the 6th). Example 58 illustrates Voicing P4 applied to major, dominant, minor, and minor 7th, ♭5 chords. Voicing P4 should already be very familiar to you because it was used in its four-note configuration for the V7 chord of Pattern P2. Note that the 7th is the top note of the voicing.

Example 58

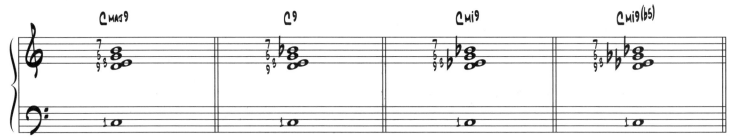

Example 59 illustrates ii-V-I Pattern P4 Major. Notice that the V7 chord in this pattern uses Voicing P2 in a five-note configuration.

Example 59

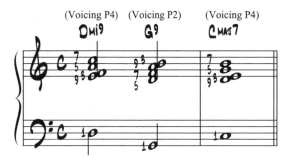

Pattern P4 Minor is illustrated in Example 60. As with Pattern P3 Minor, the V7 chord of this pattern contains two altered notes, ♭9 and ♭13.

Example 60

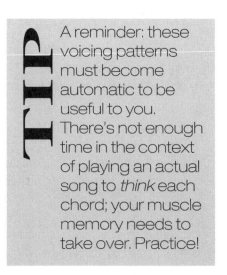

A reminder: these voicing patterns must become automatic to be useful to you. There's not enough time in the context of playing an actual song to *think* each chord; your muscle memory needs to take over. Practice!

Exercise 43
Major

Play Patterns P4 Major and P4 Minor as written in Exercise 43. Your goal is to be able to play them perfectly at ♩ = 88.

Minor

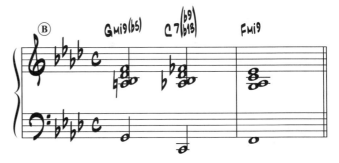

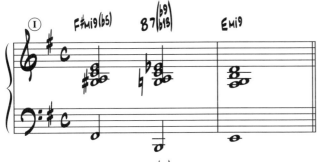

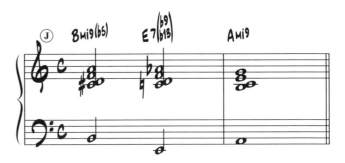

MIXING AND MATCHING THE PATTERNS (P1, P2, P3, and P4)

Now, you'll combine Patterns P3 and P4 within a song just as you did with Patterns P1 and P2 in Chapter 4. This will allow your playing to sound smoother and more connected while also giving you more practice at playing the new patterns. The goal in combining any patterns is to minimize the repositioning of hands as much as possible to achieve better voice leading.

Play the "The Shadow of Your Smile" as written in Exercise 44. (See Exercise 41 on pg. 75 to reference the song's melody.) This version utilizes a combination of Patterns P3 and P4.

Exercise 44
"Shadow of Your Smile"

Music by JOHNNY MANDEL
Lyric by PAUL FRANCIS WEBSTER

At this point in your study and practice of jazz piano, you should be comfortable playing Patterns P1 (5th on top), P2 (3rd on top), P3 (9th on top), and P4 (7th on top) in any key. You'll now use all four of these familiar patterns by mixing and matching them within a song. Fluency at combining these four patterns is the key to achieving the smoothest possible voice leading.

Play versions a and b of "The Shadow of Your Smile" as written in Exercise 45. Notice that each version utilizes a different combination of Voicing and Patterns P1, P2, P3 and P4. The shifting between these positions helps to create interest and connect the chords seamlessly.

Exercise 45a
"Shadow of Your Smile"

LISTEN Track 7
Music by JOHNNY MANDEL
Lyric by PAUL FRANCIS WEBSTER

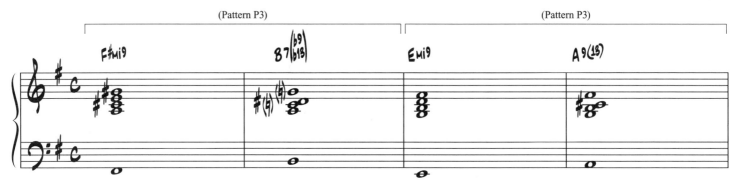

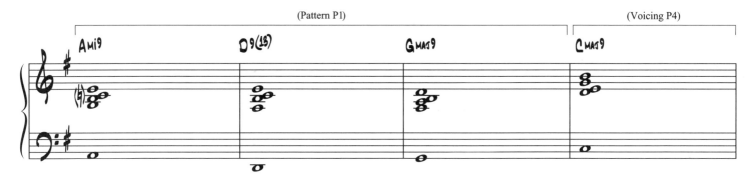

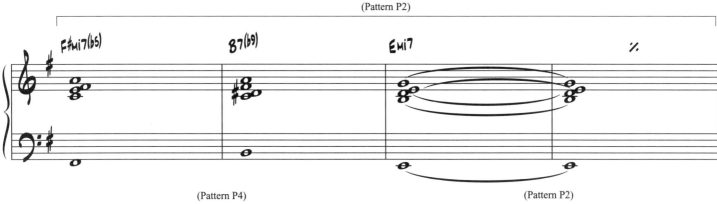

Exercise 45b
"Shadow of Your Smile"

Track 7
Music by JOHNNY MANDEL
Lyric by PAUL FRANCIS WEBSTER

Additional Practice:

Play through Etude 8 in Appendix I and listen to the corresponding CD Track 18. Also, experiment with first mixing and matching Patterns P3, and P4 within a song, then mixing and matching all four Patterns (P1, P2, P3 and P4). Good song choices include "Alone Together," "Devil May Care," "Laura" and "On A Clear Day."

Chapter 8 Open Voicings

> **GOAL:** Study and practice open position, five-note chord voicings, and play them with an even distribution of notes between the two hands. The use of open voicings will greatly increase the possibilities for interest and variety in your playing.

DROP 2 VOICINGS

Up to this point you've played three or four-note block chords *(close position)* in the right hand and a single note in the left hand, exclusively. Though this voicing style is useful, especially for rhythmic styles, it does have limitations. For example: you will eventually run out of available fingers to play an expanded palette of voicings, and the one-dimensional texture will become tiring to the ear. *Open position* voicings allow for easier integration of color notes and free up fingers to play broken chords and passing notes. (See Chapter 9, Pianistic Texture, pgs. 96, 97.)

It's easy to convert (close position) block voicings to open position by moving the second note from the top down an octave as in Example 61. This method of devising open voicings is commonly referred to as *Drop 2*. Notice that a redistribution of notes between the hands is required—two notes played in the left hand and two or more notes in the right.

STUDY Example 61

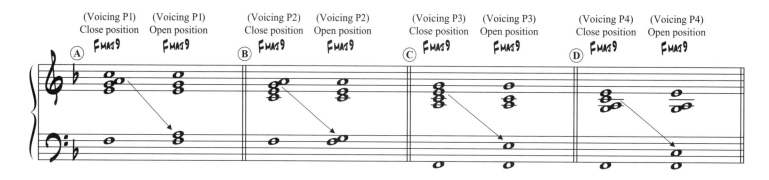

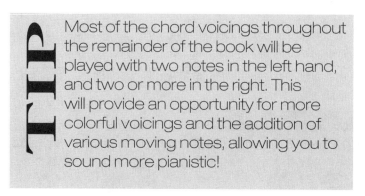

Most of the chord voicings throughout the remainder of the book will be played with two notes in the left hand, and two or more in the right. This will provide an opportunity for more colorful voicings and the addition of various moving notes, allowing you to sound more pianistic!

In practical use, Drop 2 works best with Patterns P1 and P3—you can count on these patterns to sound good in both major and minor key open voicing configuration. Pattern P4 also works well in most cases but is not as commonly used as Patterns P1 and P3. Pattern P2 in five-note open configuration can be problematic, especially when a 9th is used on minor 7th or minor 7th, ♭5 chords.

Example 62 illustrates two versions of Pattern P2 Minor in five-note Drop 2 configuration. Version A does not work well because use of the 9th on the imi7 and iimi7(♭5) chords creates excessive dissonance. Version B of this pattern sounds better because the 9th is eliminated on the minor chords.

STUDY Example 62

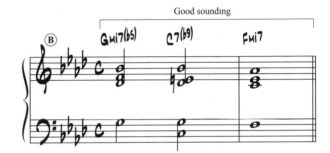

Notice the use of major and minor 6th chords in Exercise 46. Major 6th chords are generally interchangeable with major 7th chords. Similarly, minor 6th chords are generally interchangeable with minor 7th chords when they function as the "i" chord as in Exercise 46. When a minor chord functions as ii-7, iii-7 or vi-7 in a progression, the minor 7th chord is used.

Play open voicing Patterns P1 and P3 as written in Exercise 46. Your goal is to be able to play them perfectly at ♩ = 88. Feel free to experiment with the use of other color notes of your choice. Since the distribution of two notes in the left hand and three in the right is new for you, it may require a little extra practice time. Hang in there!

Exercise 46
Pattern P1 Major

Pattern P1 Minor

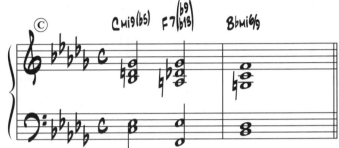

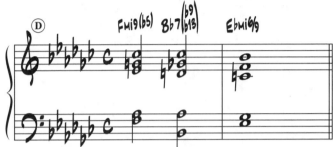

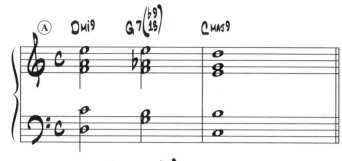

Pattern P3 Major

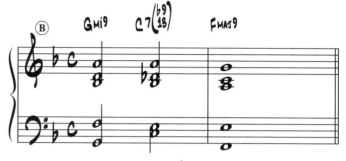
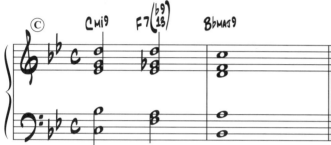

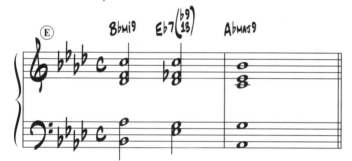
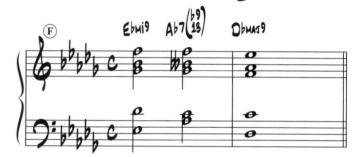
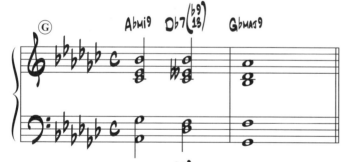

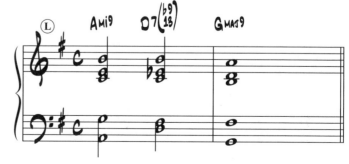

Pattern P3 Minor

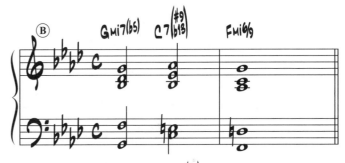

Optionally, you may wish to practice playing Patterns P2 and P4 in open position as you did with Patterns P1 and P3 in Exercise 46. Always use your ears to determine which voicing/color note combinations sound best. To remedy a voicing that does not sound good, try voicing the chord in close position, adjusting the choice of color notes, or using a four-note configuration.

Now, apply open voicings to a song. Exercise 47 features a combination of Voicings P1, P2, P3 and P4 in open position, though Voicings P1 and P3 are used for most of the chords in this exercise. Each individual voicing position is identified for your reference.

Exercise 47
"Shadow of Your Smile"

LISTEN Track 8

Music by JOHNNY MANDEL
Lyric by PAUL FRANCIS WEBSTER

TIP

There are important considerations when applying open voicings to a song, particularly in regard to the piano register. In general, when playing lower on the keyboard the chords should be less dense and have fewer notes with wider intervals between notes. In general, you'll want to use a combination of four and five-note voicings in both open and close position.

Additional Practice:

Play through Etudes 9 and 10 in Appendix I and listen to the corresponding CD Tracks 19 and 20. Also, experiment with playing Drop 2 voicings on songs of your choice. Good song choices include "Alone Together," "Devil May Care," "Laura" and "On A Clear Day."

NON-FORMULAIC OPEN VOICINGS

There are many other open voicing possibilities that are not based on Voicings P1, P2, P3 or P4 or derived from a specific formula such as Drop 2. The use of these non-formulaic open voicings will give you a great deal of flexibility and creative choice, but also require you to think more!

Some non-formulaic voicings are very similar to the Voicing P1, P2, P3 and P4 prototypes, departing from them only slightly as in Example 63.

STUDY **Example 63**

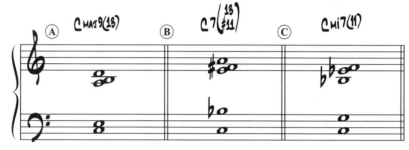

Example 64 illustrates two examples of *Quartal* voicings. The term Quartal is a reference to voicings that are built primarily in perfect fourth intervals.

STUDY **Example 64**

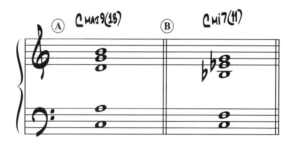

Surprisingly, the omission of the 3rd of the chord can work well in certain chord voicings. Notice in Example 65 that the overall sound of each chord quality (major 7th and minor 7th, ♭5 respectively) is still clear.

STUDY **Example 65**

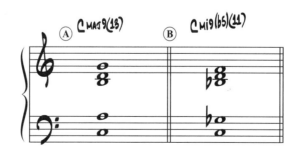

Six-note voicings open up a whole new realm of possibilities for the addition of color notes and full-ness of sound. Example 66 illustrates some of the many options.

Example 66

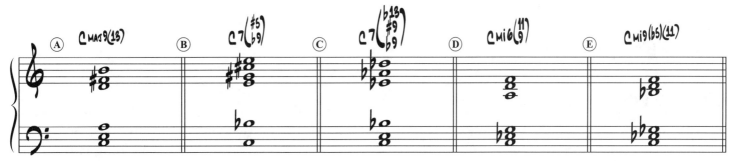

A quick and easy method of creating interesting chord voicings is to superimpose one chord over another as in Example 67. These voicings are referred to as *polychords*.

Example 67

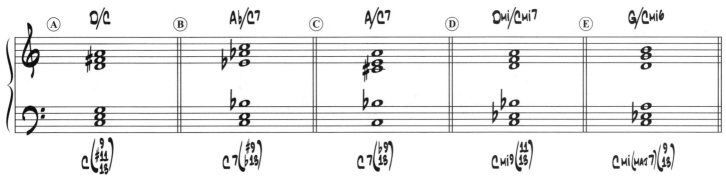

TIP For a complete Catalog of Voicings in all shapes, sizes and kinds, go to **www.micheleweir.com**. The Resources page offers a variety of educational tools and information. Refer to the Catalog of Voicings when you're playing a tune in accompaniment or solo piano style to discover new and interesting voicings.

Chapter **9** Pianistic Texture

GOAL: Practice specific exercises for breaking up chord voicings in a pianistic way and adding passing tones to create interest and maintain a sense of motion. The integration of texture to your playing is an important step toward becoming a well-rounded jazz pianist.

BROKEN CHORDS

There are a number of easy methods to add texture to your playing by breaking up the solid chord voicings you've played in previous chapters. These techniques will go a long way in helping you sound more pianistic—smooth, connected, varied, and musical.

Example 68 illustrates five specific broken chord techniques.

 STUDY Example 68

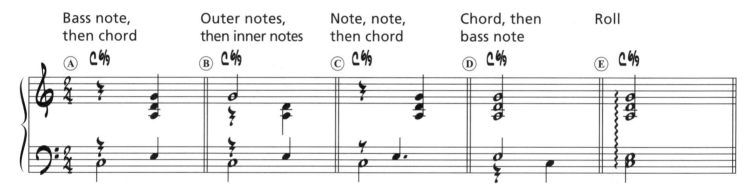

Play the patterns in Exercise 48 by transposing to all keys. Note that the exercises below are based on Exercise 46 from Chapter 8—refer to Exercise 46 on pgs. 88–91 as necessary when transposing. Your goal is to be able to play them perfectly at ♩ = 72. Remember that all short exercises should be practiced by starting in a different key each day.

 PLAY Exercise 48

PASSING NOTES

Passing notes are a decorative element that help to connect the chords and maintain a linear musical flow. Numerous songs already have built-in passing notes as dictated by the chord symbols. Common examples of passing note movement built into songs include the ascending 5th as illustrated in Example 69.

Example 69
STUDY **"It Never Entered My Mind"**

Another common example of passing note movement in songs is the descending 7th as illustrated in Example 70.

Example 70
STUDY **"My Funny Valentine"**

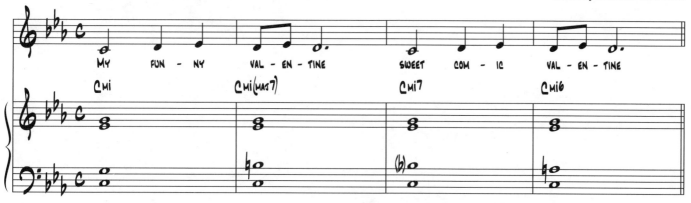

You can apply similar passing notes to other songs by adding them wherever the harmony is static for one or two bars—providing the passing notes don't interfere with the song's melody.

The 4–3 suspension occurring on a dominant seventh chord is another very useful type of passing movement that helps promote a sense of forward motion in the chord progression. Example 71 illustrates two examples.

STUDY **Example 71**

> **TIP**
> Don't confuse suspended 4ths with added 11ths. Although they both represent the same note of the scale, the two *function* differently: the 11th is *added* to minor family chords, whereas the sus 4th temporarily *replaces* the 3rd on major and dominant family chords. Adding to the potential confusion is that the chord symbol "C11" is commonly used to indicate a major or dominant 7th chord with a suspended 4th.

Extensions can pass from a natural to an altered form resulting in inner or melodic passing notes, as illustrated in Example 72. The most common examples are the movement from 9th to ♭9th, ♯9th to ♭9th, or 13th to ♭13th on dominant 7th chords. As mentioned previously, altered extensions (♭9th or ♭13th) have a strong tendency to resolve down a half-step.

Example 72

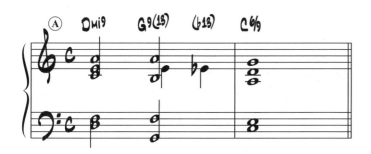

Melodic passing notes are another creative option. This type of passing movement helps to provide continuity between the chord voicings by using the top note of each chord to help construct a cohesive melodic line. Melodic passing notes should work in tandem with your chord voicings; *the final note of the fill should coincide with the top note of a chord voicing most of the time*. Notice in Example 73 that the passing notes are diatonic (within the scale,) and usually occur on the weak beats of the measure.

Example 73

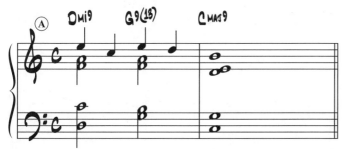

Passing notes can also occur in the bass voice, again, helping to provide connection and continuity between the chord changes. Notice in Example 74 that the passing bass notes move either diatonically or chromatically, and always lead to a chord tone.

Example 74

When playing pianistically, the top note of each voicing or passing line is like a melody. These melodic lines should be played to sound a little louder than the rest of the chord, making them *sing*. Attention to this important detail will add sophistication to your playing. Listen to the examples on the CD Tracks 21-24 and notice how clearly the chords ring with the top note sounding more prominently than the others

In Exercise 49 you'll play a combination of broken chords and passing notes. Transpose each of the exercises to play them in all keys. As with Exercise 48, *the exercises below are based on Exercise 46 from Chapter 8, pgs. 88–91.* Your goal is to be able to play them perfectly at ♩ = 66.

 Exercise 49

Major

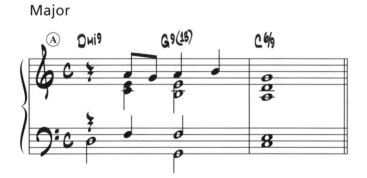

Minor

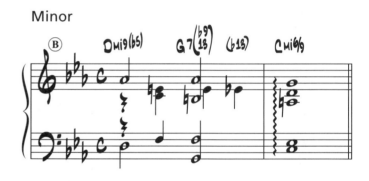

Major

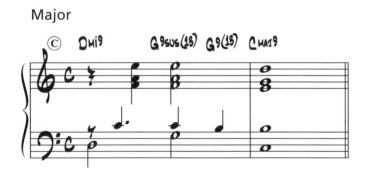

Minor

Too many spices spoil the soup. Intersperse a few simple block chords in between the various broken chords and passing notes for contrast.

Now, play a combination of broken chords and passing notes within a song in Exercise 50. Blending the two techniques together will help you achieve a good linear flow and more pianistic style of playing. The specific broken chord technique or passing note style is identified above each measure. Note that the voicings are based upon the voicings from Exercise 47 (Chapter 8, pg. 92). Make every effort to bring out the sense of melodic line in the top voice.

Example 50
"The Shadow of Your Smile"   **LISTEN Track 9**

Music by JOHNNY MANDEL
Lyric by PAUL FRANCIS WEBSTER

Additional Practice:

Play through Etudes 11 and 12 in Appendix I and listen to the corresponding CD Tracks 21 and 22. Also, using a song of your choice, try integrating various broken chords and passing notes into your playing. Good song choices include "Alone Together," "Devil May Care," "Laura" and "On A Clear Day."

Chapter 10 Playing The Tune!

GOAL: Learn solo piano style playing by modifying Voicings P1, P2, P3 and P4 to incorporate the song's melody and add fills. You will have more creative choice in the construction of your voicings and less adherence to voicing patterns than in previous chapters which dealt exclusively with accompaniment styles of playing.

HARMONIZING THE MELODY

Examples 75–78 illustrate a step-by-step process for constructing voicings beneath a given melody and chord progression.

1. Harmonize the melody only on a strong beat or in places where the chord changes. First determine if the melody note to be harmonized is a chord tone. If so, harmonize it using Voicing P1, P2, P3 or P4, whichever happens to have that melody note on top. Other melody notes should be left unharmonized to act as passing tones. Notice in Example 75 that a chord is played on beat one to establish the harmonic context before the melody begins.

 **Example 75**
"Lady Is A Tramp"

Words by LORENZ HART
Music by RICHARD RODGERS

TIP Avoid doubling notes in your chord voicings except when necessary, for purposes of good voice leading for example. Example 75 illustrates the effective use of a doubled note on the G7(13) chord.

2. If the given melody note is not a chord tone but *is* an appropriate color note, then modify the voicing by changing the top note as in Example 76 or adding an extra note in the top voice.

Example 76
"Prelude to a Kiss"

Words by IRVING MILLS and IRVING GORDON
Music by DUKE ELLINGTON

3. Avoid playing a half-step between the top two notes. This will detract from the melody. Notice in Example 77 that omission of the 9th on the Gmi7 chord is necessary to alleviate a half-step clash that would detract from the melody.

Example 77
"Alone Together"

Lyrics by HOWARD DIETZ
Music by ARTHUR SCHWARTZ

4. Once solid block chords have been established, add broken chords and passing tones just as you did in the accompaniment style of playing. Example 78 illustrates "Alone Together" as harmonized in Example 77, this time with broken chords and passing notes.

Example 78
"Alone Together"

Lyrics by HOWARD DIETZ
Music by ARTHUR SCHWARTZ

5. Always strive for good voice leading in chord voicings, making every effort to minimize hand movement thru the smooth connection of chords. Periodically it will be necessary to lift your hands and reposition them to a new location at the piano, for example when the melody makes a wide intervallic leap.

Play the first 8 bars of "You Go To My Head" as written in Exercise 51. I recommend when first learning to harmonize a melody that you play in block chord style, with no broken chords or passing notes as in this exercise. Once correct voicings have been established it will be much easier to add pianistic texture. Always strive to bring out the melody when you play.

Exercise 51
"You Go To My Head"

Words by HAVEN GILLESPIE
Music by J. FRED COOTS

FILLS

Song melodies are sometimes active and other times at rest, particularly at the end of a phrase. The moments of melodic rest provide an opportunity to inject brief melodic fills to keep things interesting and help propel the song forward. Melodic fills can be constructed in the same way as melodic passing notes: connect the chords via passing notes to create a simple melody in the top voice.

Melodic fills can be arpeggiated as illustrated in Example 79.

Example 79
"What Is This Thing Called Love"

Words and Music by COLE PORTER

Example 80 illustrates melodic fills that pass in scalar motion from one chord to the next.

Example 80
"What Is This Thing Called Love"

Words and Music by COLE PORTER

Melodic fills can also pass in irregular shapes from one chord to the next as in Example 81.

Example 81
"What Is This Thing Called Love"

Words and Music by COLE PORTER

Short and simple melodic fills are often the best; avoid playing too many notes. Try singing along with your fills in practice to help make them lyrical. Melodic fills often work well in conjunction with slight alterations of the melody.

Play "You Go To My Head" again, as written in Exercise 52. This version of the song includes broken chords, passing notes and melodic fills. Note that Exercise 52 is based on Exercise 51 (pg. 104).

Exercise 52
"You Go To My Head"

LISTEN Track 10

Words by HAVEN GILLESPIE
Music by J. FRED COOTS

MELODIC TROUBLEMAKERS

The unpredictable twists and turns in a song's melody and chord progression are what make the tune distinctive. Without occasional melodic or harmonic surprises, all tunes would all end up sounding the same! It is these twists and turns however that can also make the song a challenge to play. Sometimes a melody note simply does not seem to fit with the given chord symbol, raising the question of how it should be harmonized. Below are a few examples of melodic *troublemakers* and methods for resolving them.

    1. Accented passing note

An *accented passing note* is a passing note occurring on a strong beat. When the accented passing note is not a chord tone or appropriate color note of the corresponding chord symbol, it can be problematic. One solution in this situation is to alter the chord type to accommodate the note. An alternative is to simply allow the note to be superimposed over the incompatible chord symbol despite the momentary clash. This solution works only when the problematic note is of a very short duration. Note the accented passing notes (circled) in Example 82.

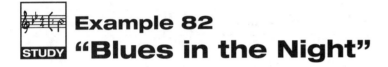

Example 82
"Blues in the Night"

Words by JOHNNY MERCER
Music by HAROLD ARLEN

    2. Blues Scale

The *blues scale* is a unique scale that is commonly used with blues and other chord progressions. Example 83 illustrates the blues scale in the key of C.

Example 83

Many jazz tunes reference portions of the blues scale in the melody. This scale has such a strong, bluesy character that it can sound good on virtually any progression, overriding the need for every melody note to "fit" correctly with every chord. In other words, a single blues scale can be juxtaposed over a chord progression even when a note or two momentarily clashes. The note G♭ in the 4th measure of Example 84 for example would normally be considered incompatible with the given chord symbol, yet it works here because it's part of a melodic phrase based on the blues scale.

Example 84
"Since I Fell For You"

Words and Music by BUDDY JOHNSON

3. Anticipation

Sometimes a problematic melody note is actually an anticipation of the next chord. In this case the solution is to harmonize the note as the chord it's anticipating as in Example 85.

Example 85
"A Foggy Day"

Music and Lyrics by
GEORGE GERSHWIN and IRA GERSHWIN

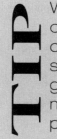

When a chord symbol appears only as a single letter of the alphabet, it is an indication to play a triad. In most cases however you could substitute a major sixth or major seventh chord for the triad—these three chord types are generally interchangeable providing they work well with the melody. For example the F(9) chord in Example 85 could be played as F6(9) or Fmaj9.

4. Faulty Chord Symbols

Lead sheets occasionally have faulty chord symbols. When in doubt, double-check the chord in question with another source, or, alter the chord to your best educated guess. Example 86 illustrates common examples of mislabeled or extraneous chords.

STUDY Example 86

Correct notes in chord but wrong root

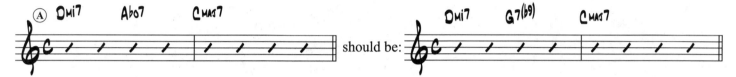

Extraneous chord symbols

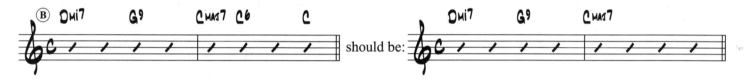

Additional Practice:

Play through Etudes 13 and 14 in Appendix I and listen to the corresponding CD Tracks 23 and 24. Also, using songs of your choice, try harmonizing the melody and adding fills. Good song choices include "All the Things You Are," "Get Out of Town," "Our Love is Here To Stay" and "When I Fall in Love."

APPENDIX I: ETUDES

The following etudes allow for additional practice at playing songs in all three of the styles covered in this book: (1) rubato accompaniment style, (2) rhythmic accompaniment style, and (3) solo piano style. *It is strongly recommended that you play each etude immediately after working thru its corresponding chapter.* The etudes with metronome markings should be played in tempo, all others should be considered rubato. I recommend that you analyze and bracket the voicings and patterns (P1, P2, P3 or P4) used for each etude. For the accompaniment etudes, you may want to sing the melody yourself, have a friend play or sing it, or disregard it entirely to focus exclusively on your piano playing.

TIP All of the songs in Appendix I are based on the chord progressions of well-known jazz standards.

Etude 1: Rainy Day

Etude 2: You Love Me

Etude 3: The Moon Has Risen

Etude 4: Lullaby for the Birds

Etude 5: A Fool's Day

Etude 6: In Love I Will Fall

Etude 7: Time and Time Again

Etude 8: Far Away a Long Time Ago

Etude 9: What Could Be New?

Etude 10: Don't Tell Me

Etude 11: You Are All Things

Etude 12: Valentine's Day

Etude 13: Embraceable You

Music and Lyrics by
GEORGE GERSHWIN and IRA GERSHWIN

Etude 14: A Foggy Day

Music and Lyrics by
GEORGE GERSHWIN and IRA GERSHWIN

APPENDIX II: CHORD SYMBOLS AND COLOR NOTES CHART

Diagram 6 illustrates various chord types and color note configurations along with their corresponding chord symbols. As mentioned previously, there is currently no standardization for chord symbol nomenclature. It is common to encounter various different chord symbols used to represent the same chord type. Therefore, familiarity with all of them is an asset!

The chord symbols in Diagram 6 are categorized into two groups, *Recommended* and *Alternates*. Chord symbols in the Recommended column are preferred by the author and publisher, though they are certainly not the only viable choices. Chord symbols in the Alternates column represent only a sample of other possible options for each chord. There are so many different choices it would not be feasible to list them all.

Diagram 6

Chord Type	Color Notes	Recommended Chord Symbols	Alternate Chord Symbols
Major Triad	----	C	CTRIAD, CΔ, CMA, CMAJ
Major Triad	9	C(9) C ADD9	C2, CADD2, CΔ(9), CMAJ(9)
Major Triad	#5	C(#5)	C+, C(+5), CAUG
Major 6th	----	C6	CADD6, CMAJ6, CMA6
Major 6th	9	C6/9	C6(9), C69, C6/9, CADD6/9, CMAJ6/9
Major 6th	#11 (or b5)	C6(#11)	C6(+11), CADD6(+11)
Major 7th	----	CMAJ7	CMA7, CΔ7, CΔ, CM7, CΔ7
Major 7th	9	CMAJ9	CMAJ7(9), CΔ9, CM9
Major 7th	#11	CMAJ7(#11)	CMAJ7(+11), CΔ7(+11), CM7(#11), CΔ
Major 7th	#5	CMAJ7(#5)	CMAJ7(+5), CΔ7(+5), CM7AUG, C7(#5)
Major 7th	13	CMAJ7(13)	CMAJ13, CΔ13, CM7(13)
Major 7th	9, #11	CMAJ9(#11)	CMAJ7(9/+11), CMAJ9(+11), CΔ9(#11), CM9(#11)
Major 7th	9, 13	CMAJ9(13)	CMAJ13, CMAJ7(9/13), CΔ13, CM9(13)
Major 7th	9, #11, 13	CMAJ9(#11/13)	CMAJ13, Δ/CMAJ7, CΔ9(+11/13), CM9(#11/13)
Dominant 7th	----	C7	CDOM7
Dominant 7th	9	C9	C7(9), C7ADD9, CDOM9
Dominant 7th	b9	C7(b9)	C7(-9), C7ALT
Dominant 7th	#9	C7(#9)	C7(+9), C7(b10)
Dominant 7th	#11 (or b5)	C7(#11)	C7(+11), C7(-5), C7(+4)
Dominant 7th	13	C7(13)	C13, CDOM13
Dominant 7th	b13	C7(b13)	C7(-13), C7ALT
Dominant 7th	#5	C7(#5)	C+7, C7(+5), CAUG7
Dominant 7th	9, #11 (or b5)	C9(#11)	C9(-5), C7(9/+11)
Dominant 7th	9, 13	C9(13)	C13, C7(9/13), CDOM13
Dominant 7th	9, b13	C9(b13)	C9(-13), C+9, CAUG9
Dominant 7th	b9, #11 (or b5)	C7(b9/#11)	C7(-9/+11), C7(-9/-5), C7ALT, F#/C7
Dominant 7th	b9, 13	C7(b9/13)	C13(b9), A/C7, C7(-9/13)
Dominant 7th	#9, 13	C7(#9/13)	C13(#9), C7(+9/13)
Dominant 7th	b9, b13 (or #5)	C7(b9/b13)	C7(-9/-13), C+7(b9), C7ALT
Dominant 7th	#9, b13 (or #5)	C7(#9/b13)	C7(+9/-13), C+7(#9), Ab/C7, C7ALT
Dominant 7th	9, #11, 13	C9(#11/13)	C13, C9(#11/13), D/C7

TIP

Each chord symbol in the Diagram 6 Alternates column was taken from an actual piece of music or educational publication. Don't be surprised if you see a few unusual chord symbols there!

Chord Type	Color Notes	Recommended Chord Symbols	Alternate Chord Symbols
Dominant 7th Sus	----	C7sus	C7sus4, C4, C11
Dominant 7th Sus	9	C9sus	C7$\binom{9}{sus}$, Gmi7/C, B♭/C
Dominant 7th Sus	♭9	C7sus(♭9)	C7sus(-9)
Dominant 7th Sus	13	C7sus(13)	C7$\binom{13}{sus}$, C13sus
Dominant 7th Sus	9, 13	C9sus(13)	C13sus, C Dom13 sus
Dominant 7th Sus	♭9, 13	C7sus$\binom{13}{♭9}$	C$\binom{13(♭9)}{sus}$, C7sus$\binom{-9}{13}$
Minor Triad	----	Cmi	Cmin, C-, Cm, C-triad
Minor Triad	9	Cmi9, Cmi add9	Cmi2, C-(9), Cm add9
Minor Triad	#5	Cmi(#5)	Cmi+, Cmi(+5), C-(#5), Cm+5
Minor 6th	----	Cmi6	Cmi add6, C-6, Cm6, Cmin6
Minor 6th	9	Cmi6/9	Cmi6(9), Cmi69, Cmin$\frac{6}{9}$, C-6/9, Cm6/9
Minor 6th	11	Cmi6(11)	C-6(11), Cm6(11)
Minor 6th	9, 11	Cmi6/9(11)	Cmin6$\binom{9}{11}$, Cm6/9(11), Cmi6$\binom{9}{11}$, C-6/9(11)
Minor 7th	----	Cmi7	Cmin7, C-7, Cm7
Minor 7th	9	Cmi9	Cmi7(9), C-9, Cmin9, Cm7(9)
Minor 7th	11	Cmi7(11)	Cmi11, C-9(11), Cm9(11), Cmin$\frac{9}{11}$
Minor 7th	13	Cm7(13)	Cmi13, Cm7(13), C-7(13)
Minor 7th	9, 11	Cmi9(11)	Cmi7$\binom{9}{11}$, C-9(11), Cmin11
Minor 7th	9, 11, 13	Cmi9$\binom{11}{13}$	Cmi13, C-9$\binom{11}{13}$, Cm13
Minor/Major 7th	----	Cmi(maj7)	Cmin(Δ7), Cmi/ma7, C-(maj), Cmin(+7)
Minor/Major 7th	9	Cmi9(maj7)	Cmi△9, C mi/ma9
Minor 7th, ♭5	----	Cø7, Cmi7(♭5)	C-7♭5, Cmin7(-5), Cm7(♭5)
Minor 7th, ♭5	9	Cø9, Cmi9(♭5)	Cmi9(-5), C-9♭5
Minor 7th, ♭5	11	Cø7(11), Cmi(♭5)(11)	C-11(♭5), Cmi7$\binom{-5}{11}$
Minor 7th, ♭5	9, 11	Cø9(11), Cmi9(♭5)(11)	C-11(♭5), Cmin9$\binom{-5}{11}$
Diminished Triad	----	Co, Cdim	----
Diminished Triad	9	Co(9), Cdim(9)	Co(add9)
Diminished 7th	----	Co7, Cdim7	----
Diminished 7th	9	Co9, Cdim9	Co7(9), Cdim7(9)
Diminished 7th	Other Extensions	Extensions beyond the 9th are rarely written with this chord type.	Co7(add maj7), Cdim11, Co9(♭13)

GLOSSARY

Accented passing note: Accented passing note: A passing note occurring on a strong beat. pg. 103.

Altered notes: Chord tones or extensions that are raised or lowered by a half step: ♭9, ♯9, ♭5, ♯5, ♯11, ♭13. pg. 28.

Bar: A measure.

Block chords: Four-note chords voiced in close position with all notes played at the same time, i.e., not arpeggiated. pg. 19.

Blues scale: A scale that is commonly used with blues and other chord progressions. It consists of the 1, ♭3, 4, ♯4, 5 and ♭7 scale degrees. pg. 107.

Bossa nova: A Brazilian rhythmic style that has a straight-eighth feel, as opposed to the swing eighths in swing feel. pg. 57.

Changes: Slang for "chord changes."

Chart: A lead sheet that contains arranging elements such as an intro, endings and rhythmic kicks.

Chord function: A reference to the harmonic role of a given chord within a progression. For example in the key of C, a Dmi7 chord functions as the ii-7 chord. However, in the key of F, a Dmi7 chord functions as the vi-7 chord. pg. 28.

Chorus: A term commonly used by jazz musicians to indicate one time thru the form of the song. pg. 54.

Circle of 5ths: A circular diagram illustrating all 12 key centers in clockwise succession by the interval of a perfect fifth. pg.16.

Close position voicings: Voicings where the notes are in the closest possible position to each other. pg. 86.

Comping: Playing rootless chord voicings in a rhythmic way. Comping is short for accompanying or complementing . pg. 50.

Damper Pedal: See Sustain pedal.

Diatonic: Chords and notes that occur naturally, with no alteration, within a certain major or minor scale. pg. 23.

Drop 2: A method of devising open voicings by moving the second note below the top of a close position chord down an octave. pg 86.

Even eighths: See straight eighths pg. 57.

Extensions: Non-chord tones, specifically the 9th, 11th and 13th scale degrees, added to chords for interest. pg. 20.

Fake book: A compilation of lead sheets notating melody, chord symbols, and lyrics if applicable.

Gig: Slang for professional music performance, usually referring to a performance in a club or private party.

Harmonize: To create chord structure or voicings for a given melody. pgs 16, 102.

Jazz ballad: A rhythmic style that is characterized by a slow, steady feeling of four beats per measure, usually with a slight underlying eighth note triplet feeling. Also referred to as "Ballad Tempo." pg. 62.

Jazz standard: Well-known, commonly performed songs in the repertoire of most professional jazz musicians.

Jazz waltz: A rhythmic feel in 3/4 meter. It differs from a traditional waltz in that the eighth notes are swing eighths just like in swing feel. pg. 61.

Lead sheet: Music that is notated with melody, chord symbols and if applicable, lyrics.

Open position voicings: Voicings in which the notes are not all in the closest possible position to each other; there is more intervallic space between at least one pair of notes. pg. 86.

Pianistic: A style of playing that incorporates broken chords and passing notes to solid chord voicings, giving them greater interest, sense of motion, and linear flow. pg. 96.

Pivot chords: A link between one key center with the next, helping to smooth the transition during a harmonic modulation. pg. 44.

Polychord: The superimposition of one chord over another, played simultaneously. For example, D/C7. pg. 95.

Quartal voicing: A voicing built primarily in perfect fourth intervals. pg. 94.

Quick fix voicing: Often referred to as a shell voicing (for purposes of this book), consists of the 3rd and 7th of each chord (or 3rd and 6th as dictated by the chord symbol) in the right hand, and the root of the chord in the left. pgs. 18, 19.

Relative major: Each minor key and scale corresponds to a relative major key and scale that shares the same notes and key signature. For example, the F major scale contains the same notes and key signature as the D natural minor scale. F major is referred to as the relative major of D minor. pg. 12.

Relative minor: Each major key and scale corresponds to a relative minor key and scale that shares the same notes and key signature. For example, the D natural minor scale contains the same notes and key signature as the F major scale. D minor is referred to as the relative minor of F major. pg. 12.

Rhythm changes: Slang referring to the popular chord progression to the song, "I Got Rhythm."

Rootless voicings: Chord voicings that do not contain the root of the chord. Rootless voicings are typically used by pianists and guitar players when working with a bass player. pg. 50.

Rubato: With no tempo; freely.

Samba: Like the bossa nova, samba is a rhythmic style that originates from Brazil. It differs from bossa nova in that it has a "2" feel in which each measure feels like it has two beats per measure, not four. The bass line consists primarily of half notes. pg. 62.

Secondary dominant: A dominant seventh chord a perfect fifth above the chord it's progressing to, regardless of the key of the song. pg. 45.

Shell voicing: See Quick fix voicing.

Slash chord: A chord played over a single bass note that is different than the root of that chord. (For example: G-7/C) pg. 48.

Straight eighths: Also known as even-eighths are simply eighth notes that are played with an even subdivision, not swung. pg. 57.

Standard: See "Jazz standard."

Substitution: The replacement of one chord for another in a progression for purposes of creating interest.

Sustain pedal: Also known as the damper pedal, is the piano foot pedal located on the far right. Use of the sustain pedal helps to connect the chords smoothly in legato playing. pg. 15.

Swing "2" feel: A type of swing feel where each measure feels like it has two beats per measure, and there is no walking bass line. pg. 54.

Swing "4" feel: Swing feel where the bassist plays a walking bass line, and there is a driving feeling of four beats per measure. pgs. 50, 54.

Tritone substitution: A dominant seventh chord that substitutes for the chord whose root is three whole steps (a tritone) away.

Turnarounds: Short chord progressions that often occur at the end of a song to provide a harmonic link back to the beginning of the song. Also referred to as a turnback. pg. 22.

Turnbacks: See Turnarounds.

Voice leading: The linear continuity between all voices or notes of a chord when moving from one chord to another. pg. 32.

Voicing: The arrangement of notes in a chord. pg. 18.

Walking bass line: A bass line consisting primarily of quarter notes, with the root of the chord usually played on the first beat of every new chord with arpeggiated or scalar passing notes in between. pg. 50.